THE DRIVE FOR FINANCIAL GAIN

Create a Profitable Side Business With Your Skills

and Begin Generating Income Today

BY

Chris Banning

The information herein is offered for informational purposes solely, and is universal as so. The presentation of the information is without contract or any type of guarantee assurance. The trademarks that are used are without any consent, and the publication of the trademark is without permission or backing by the trademark owner. All trademarks and brands within this book are for clarifying purposes only and are the owned by the owners themselves, not affiliated with this document.

CONTENTS

INTRODUCTION

It doesn't matter what abilities or traits you have. There is a market out there that wants to purchase your talent. All you have to do is locate that market and give them what they require your skill. Do you play any guitars? There are Millions of people around the globe that want to "play like you." Become a pianist? More individuals are waiting for you to impart your knowledge and abilities to them; there are a million. You can give piano lessons. I ought to know; for many years, I operated a "one-man-music school" in my home and taught many people how to do the same.

But what if you can sing or play the drums, trumpet, flute, or saxophone? What if you have skills in cartooning, needlepoint, camera repair, making beautiful scrapbooks, budgeting, etc. but don't perform any of the things listed above?

It's irrelevant because countless people want to learn what you know!

Perhaps there won't be many people in your hometown interested in what you do or know, but if you start a mail order business, you'll learn more than you ever thought possible. There are essentially no restrictions when browsing the internet. Knowledge-hungry people from China, India, Peru, France, Canada, and countless other nations join the online community rapidly. The fact that over 100,000 people register for an online account each day, many of whom are interested in what you offer, is astounding.

Nevertheless, refrain from starting online. Start with your own "Your-Name Local School," where you can instruct a few pupils using your learning resources. Then, add "Your-Name Mail Order School" to it. Use your newly created teaching tools to "long distance" teach a vast student body using these resources.

I've succeeded in all three; from my first student to today, tens of thousands of people worldwide I've taught. And after beginning with a straightforward 8-page guide on reading music, I now have over 500 instructional DVDs, CDs, books, cassettes, charts, and videos that are all meant to help people become better pianists and musicians.

I used to run my own "One-Man-Music-School" and teach students one-on-one, making a good living in the process. Then I discovered a method to "multiply myself" so that I could teach more than one person at once. I merely called it great; others call it "mail order." I could reach a lot more people if I published my courses, recorded them on video or cassette, and eventually put them on CDs and DVDs. Furthermore, I could teach anywhere, which is precisely what I do. You name it: Montana farmers, Florida physicians, Washington certified public accountants, Texas barbers, Kentucky homemakers, etc. Instead of simply 100 students, you may have thousands! My young friend Jermaine, who works in the same field, who has more over 80,000 email subscribers, has four times as many as I do now! Additionally, I have Dave, a charming and talented individual who is cleaning my clock in terms of marketing knowledge and technological prowess. Dave lives in my hometown. Do I worry? not in any way. There is space for all of us because demand for teachers is increasing exponentially. We can work together to forge affiliate agreements that are mutually advantageous.

Your teachings can be released as books, graphs, games, CDs, DVDs, software, cassettes, and other media. Direct mail, classified ads, accessible articles, mail order catalogues, and a number of different methods can all be used to advertise them. Although space does not permit a thorough examination of selling by mail order and direct mail, your local library probably has several excellent books on the topic. You'll become operational more quickly than you might anticipate if you immerse yourself in them for a few days. I've been doing it for 30 years and have sold millions of music and piano lessons, so I can promise you that it's not as tough as you think. There is no reason for you not to do it either!

The logical next step after starting your mail order business is to build your website. Unlike when you carry your orders to the post office and your checks to the bank, underwear is the ideal apparel. Since millions of people will be viewing your website, if you do it correctly, which I'll show you how to do, your business might EXPLODE. Previously, it wasn't easy to get a website up and running. I'll discuss a few tools you may use to quickly and cheaply create a gorgeous website.

Once you've established your teaching business, created some of your lessons on video, books, charts, DVDs, or CDs, and mastered the art of mail order marketing, it's time to grow it even further by creating your website and opening up your lessons to people all over the world. Even online teaching is possible if you choose; while I don't, a friend does, and it appears to be successful for him. Additionally, computer discs, CDs, DVDs, and various interactive media can save your musical ideas and lessons available today. In the years to come, who knows what will happen? Today, anyone who jumps into this media, or "mega information highway," will be far ahead of the competition.

What kind of income can you expect from your home company if you teach what you know? In such a title, the word "earn" is essential. You and I know money doesn't grow on trees or computers. If we want to keep anything, we must first earn it, whether we do it from home or not. Despite this, the following are some estimates based on my knowledge and that of other people I know who work in the teaching profession. This is valid for all subject areas, not just music. Since music is the subject I know the most about, I'll use that as an example.

Whether you live in a city or the country, the cost of living varies greatly depending on where you are in the country. However, if you provide half-hour lessons, you might make, on average, $50 per hour as a beginning music teacher, or about $25 each lesson. Experienced teachers can earn twice as much ($50 per lesson, $100 per hour). Additionally, as you might anticipate, some top professors earn considerably more than that. I'll give you an example that might make your mind stray: You may eliminate missed classes and steady your income by charging by the month rather than the lesson.

For instance, when I used to bill monthly in the 1970s, parents loved it because it encouraged kids to attend an hour lesson rather than a half-hour class. The student would spend 20 minutes with me, 20 minutes watching a video strip on music theory, and 20 minutes working with one of my more experienced students on the subject I had given them.

Three halves made up the hour for me. It went well between the student, the parents, and me, and they all appreciated it. With three students onboard each hour, alternating between the three "stations" mentioned above, I was making three times as much money per hour as the average teacher would! Naturally, I had to pay my "assistant teachers" (the older pupils) and buy the projector and film strips to get started. Still, once it was up and running, it was a terrific home business revenue for a minimum amount of time spent instructing music. Even though I only taught from 3 to 8 in the afternoon during those years, I had about 100 students. I could support myself full-time even though I only worked 25 hours per week or five days. Throughout the week, I also had time to expand my teaching company' mail-order division, which eventually exceeded the private instruction component.

You could quickly charge three times as much if YOU put up the same program as I did back in the 1970s since, after all, it's the 21st century and not 1974, and you might have noticed that things are a little more expensive now. (I purchased a brand-new Toyota Corolla) at the time for $1995. Add your instructor's salary to their current price for a rough estimate. Think about charging $100 per month, having three students per hour (like I did), and teaching from 3 to 8 in the evenings five days a week (like I did). Seventy-five students are obtained when 25 teaching hours are divided by three students. For each student, $100 is equivalent to $7500 monthly, or about $75 per hour. It's better than working a part-time shift at Burger Bash. You still have the entire morning and early afternoon to work on other elements of your business.

CHAPTER 1

HOW TO MAKE YOUR SKILLS A PROFITABLE SIDE BUSINESS

You already have interests and skills that people will pay for. It's all about finding them and making a side business. In this guide, we'll help you turn your thoughts and ideas into a solid way to make money.

Follow these eight steps to make a side business out of your skills that pay well.

1. Keep your skills, knowledge, and talents separate.

Look at what you have now to see what you can use to start your business. All of it is already in your head, so let's sort out what we can use by separating your skills, knowledge, and talents. Then, we can put everything together and make it work for you as a successful side gig or business you own.

The difference between what you know and what you can do

Knowledge is what you've learned from books, the news, school, and other places. Skill is how you use that knowledge. In other words, knowledge is a theory, and skills are the application of knowledge.

To be good at something, you need both knowledge and skills, but there is one big difference between knowledge and skill. Anyone can learn about a subject and gain knowledge, but some people will be better at some tasks than others just because they are naturally better at them. Think about how anyone can take an art history class, but some people just have a "good eye" for it.

What sets skills apart from talent

Talent is the natural ability to do things better than other people. Most people can learn about a subject and use it as a skill, but only a few will be good at it or have a talent for it. You can learn and practice skills, just like you can learn and practice facts, but you either have talent or don't.

You and some of your friends took a knitting class together. Even though you all learned and practised the same skill, at the end of the course, at least one person's scarf will probably be better designed and made because they have a natural talent for knitting. That doesn't mean everyone with a slightly chunky scarf should stop knitting. It means that people who make distinctive scarves without a natural talent might not want to open a scarf store.

"A winner is someone who knows what God has given him, works hard to turn those talents into skills, and then uses those skills to get what he wants."

2. Assess your talents

Get a pen and some paper and prepare to come up with ideas. Start by listing everything you're good at and like to do. Focus on things that you think are easy for you. Think about the things you're proud of, the things that people compliment you, and the things that have earned you professional recognition.

Think about whether any of these traits fit you and your skills. Are you creative? Are you very well organized?

• Hard-working?

• Do you learn quickly?

• Are you an excellent public speaker?

• Do you like animals?

Tip: Take a test of your personality, like the Meyers-Briggs. Type in your character and the careers you are interested in to help you plan your career at every stage, from choosing your first job to moving up in your company or changing careers later in life.

3. List the skills you can use to start a side business.

Now you need to narrow your list to the skills you have that other people might be willing to pay you for. If you didn't do any of these things on your first pass through the list, add them now:

1. Ask your friends what they think you're good at.

2. Talk to your former bosses and coworkers about what they thought you were good at.

3. Write down your hobbies and what you're passionate about.

4. What would you do if you had an hour to kill?

5. Make a list of the services you already pay for and the services you do for other people that they pay you for. Don't forget about everyday things that might not have made a list. Here's a list of tasks that could

be the first thing you check off your list and could remind you of a skill or talent you forgot you had.

- Walking dogs

- Cleaning the house

- Ironing

- Gardening

- Cooking

- Cleaning and detailing your car

- Working out

- Knowing a second language

- Organizing your closet

- Odd jobs or handyman jobs

Can you turn anything into a business?

Check your list carefully as you make changes. You want to make a side business out of things that come naturally to you. Check your list to see if it answers the question: How can I use this skill or hobby to help others?

Think about problems that you and other people might have in common and try to devise a solution.

4. Combine your skills and talents to come up with business ideas

Your list should now be short enough to show off your specific skills and talents that fit perfectly with a service that people need. For example, if your list said that you are good at paying attention to details and that your talents and skills include accounting and organization, you might be a good fit as a virtual assistant or bookkeeper. This could also be the right job if you do your taxes as soon as you get the forms from your employer or if you are good at doing paperwork.

Ask yourself if people need what you can do.

Make sure there's a need for your business idea in the market as you're coming up with it. For a business to get customers and do well, it needs to offer something people want. In particular, your skills should meet a need. It should help people or businesses make or save money or save time.

Doing some quick keyword research is a great way to find out what services people will value. If you know how to use SEMrush, you can find keywords based on questions to find out what people are searching for related to the service you will be offering. You can hire a freelancer for keyword research if you don't know how to do it yourself. By doing keyword research, you can find out your customers' problems and see if your skills can help them.

Target a specific group of people with your service.

Get yourself noticed. Which skills will make your business stand out in a sea of other similar companies? Let's go back to the example of a virtual bookkeeper from before. What makes you stand out in a sea of people doing the same thing?

Get specific by focusing on a particular industry or niche group. This will help you stand out when people search for your service and get noticed. In the case of the bookkeeper, you might want to market your services to freelancers, small businesses, Etsy sellers, or local businesses that are only in your area.

Have more than one way to make money.

Use your skills to their fullest and look into all possible ways to make money. Google businesses that are like yours to see if they offer services that you can also offer.

Getting back to our bookkeeper example, that shouldn't be the only way to make money. A bookkeeper could also make an online course about bookkeeping, offer different services for businesses and private households, or even offer online consultation services. Anyone can start an online course. You must record a video of yourself teaching others your skills and sharing the valuable information you already know.

5. Turn what you know into something valuable.

Now that you've chosen a business idea, the next step is to get people interested in your service and turn them into repeat customers. You can do this by finding ways to give your customers the most value, so they know that your service is the best deal.

You should think about why you use the services you do. Why do you go to those places in particular? It's because you like what they do for you. People will use your business for the same reason. Focusing on what customers want will help your business grow and add more value to your customers.

Customers want more than just the right product at the right price. There are many options on the market with these features, so customers are looking for extra value when making their choice. To stand out from the competition, get to know your customers personally. This will make them more likely to buy from you again.

Customers also want to know that they can trust and rely on a service to give them something useful. Building relationships with your customers helps them trust you and gives you a chance to talk about your experience.

#1: Know what gives your customers value.

You need to know what they find valuable to reach your customers most effectively. This is just a fancy way of saying that you need to know what they think is important, and the best way to find out is to ask them. Ask your customers or potential customers what they want from a business. Is it a low price, great customer service, or all of the above? Ask them what other services they buy or need that are similar to yours. This will help you find new business opportunities.

Going back to our example of bookkeeping, a customer might say that they need help filling out tax forms. One way to solve their problem would be to give them a sample form that shows what to write and where to write it. This could be sent directly to the client via email or put up on your website as a resource. If you gave your customers this kind of resource, it would save them time and keep them from having to figure it out on their own, which would be of great value to them.

#2: Know what you have to offer.

And now, some fancy math for business: The value a customer gets from a product or service is equal to the benefits minus the costs.

Basically, your customers will weigh how much they need what you're selling against how much it costs. This is what you do every time you buy anything.

In this equation, convenience is also essential. Getting gas is a great way to show this. Say you're in a hurry and will drive by a gas station with okay prices as you're late. You know there is a cheaper gas station, but it's not on your way. So you decide you'd rather pay more and not be late than not have the convenience. The most important thing is the ease of use, especially if your services aren't the cheapest.

"Make something people want and sell it, or be someone people need and sell yourself." Ryan Lilly

#3. Segment your audience

To use our gas station as an example again, not everyone might choose to pay more for gas. Some people don't have extra money to spare and might have to risk being late to save money. If the gas station was in a wealthy part of town, people might be able to pay a little more for the convenience, but in a poorer part of town, they might not have enough money to do that.

If you know this kind of background information about your potential customers, you can tailor your marketing to what they want and need. Putting your potential customers into groups will help you find the best way to reach out to them. Customers have different needs and things they care about. Instead of trying to reach all of your audience with the same message, find out what makes each segment tick and make your service, product, and marketing fit them. Put yourself in the shoes of your customer and then change your message to speak directly to them. Think about it this way: you wouldn't try to sell something to an adult the same way you'd try to sell it to a teenager. You'd take into account the needs of each audience and know that they're all different. If you know this and make your message as specific as you can, clients will feel like you already know what they need before they even walk through the door.

#4 Create a price that works for both of you.

Find the right price for the service you are offering. You want to make as much money as possible while still giving your customers enough value that they are happy. This way, everyone wins.

To figure this out, you need to consider your costs and time and what your customers are willing and/or able to pay for. Find out how much other people are charging for your service and set your price to be competitive. If your services are better or more convenient than your competitors, you can charge more because of the value. In other situations, you may be able to charge less than your competitors, which is a great way to attract customers to your business.

#5 Make it easy for people to buy your services or goods

Even though this seems obvious, it needs to be said anyway. When you start your own business, you need to make sure that the people you want to buy from you can find you. They have to be able to buy before they can sell. So, what do you do?

#6. Give people another way to buy

Make it as easy as possible for your customers to pay you. This could mean keeping up with the latest technology and accepting payments through all the different payment apps, or it could mean selling things on Instagram and having people who are interested in your product or service send you a direct message (often called a "DM") to set up payment.

You could offer different ways to pay, as well as home delivery or services where people can pay when they pick up or get the service. Offering a subscription option is another way to offer different ways to buy products. People will be able to "set and forget" their payment with a subscription, making it easy for them and for you.

#7: Make a pitch that fits their needs and worries.

People have changed how they buy services because of the COVID-19 crisis. Pay attention to what people are worried about and change your approach to fit. Due to the current situation, people are more likely to use contactless delivery, place orders over the phone, and do business over a video conferencing service like Zoom or Google Hangouts.

This idea isn't just about the current crisis: don't only accept payments through an app that no one uses. Find out what works best for the customer and go to them. Where is that if you don't know? Just ask your customers how you can make it as easy as possible for them to buy from you.

8. Use the power of digital to get customers interested.

Marketing will bring people to your business (figuratively, since you probably don't have a physical storefront). Take advantage of all the tools the internet has to offer to help people find you. Here are some suggestions:

#1. Create a blog

Make a blog to show your future clients who you are. Writing a blog is easy to help your clients understand who you are and what you do. Writing in a friendly and personal practice will help you get to know your clients and build trust. Also, having a blog makes you seem like an expert on the subject because it gives you a place to show off your knowledge and skills. You can always hire a freelancer to help you build a blog if you don't know how to do it yourself.

You can also teach people about your area of expertise and promote your services through your blog. Most blog platforms let you collect email addresses from readers with a form. You can make a mailing list out of the information you have ordered. Once you have your client's contact information, create a newsletter you can send them. You can use it to tell them about new things your company is doing and any sales you may have. In the same way, you can hire a freelancer to help you set up a blog if you don't know how to hire a freelancer to help you build a personalized newsletter opt-in form and make a newsletter template for you.

Also, if people are interested in the information you share on your blog, you can start charging for it and sell online courses. Online courses can be recorded in a way that is similar to a vlog, so going from your blog to vlogging to teaching your first online course is a natural progression.

#2. Facebook ads

You can use Facebook ads to promote your business on Facebook. First, you need to set up a Facebook business account. Then, you can start running ads on Facebook. The steps are easy to follow and are explained on their website, but you can also hire a freelance marketer to help you use best practices and get the best results.

You can also start running ads for a very low price so you can see if Facebook advertising is worth it in the long run before you spend more money and time on Facebook ad campaigns. Facebook also lets you test your ads using A/B testing and analytics, so you can find out exactly who they are reaching and who they are aimed at. This is important if you want to market to a specific segmented audience.

#3. Google local ads

Use Google local ads to find people in your area and advertise directly to them. People in the area you serve will see your ads, and creating a Google ad is low-risk because you only pay for it if someone clicks on it. If you make an ad and no one clicks on it, you haven't wasted any money.

Prices for ads are flexible, and rates are said to start as low as $1 per click. If your new business is taking up most of your time and attention, it might be a good idea to hire a freelancer to run your ad campaigns so you can focus on other things. You'll save time and energy to focus on other parts of your business. At the same time, you'll ensure your ads reach the most people possible, making the most of your time and money.

#4. Expand your social media presence

Make sure you're on social media so your customers can find you and learn more about what you do or sell. People often look at the business owner's social media accounts to determine if a product is a natural or a scam. You can build trust and credibility by not only showing off your business on social media but also by showing off yourself.

Think about your future customers and figure out the best way to reach them on social media. If your audience is mostly older people, you should have a strong presence on Facebook. If your audience is mostly millennials, you might want to have a stronger presence on Instagram. On TikTok, you can find users who are even younger. Find businesses that offer services like yours and follow all of the people who like and follow those businesses. This will get people to check out your account, which will help you get more followers. By responding to their comments and liking their posts, you can build a digital relationship with them that can lead to sales.

Keeping up with social media can take up a lot of time. There is a reason why large, wellknown companies have large social media teams that handle branding, copywriting, content creation, graphic design, and scheduling to make sure the company is running at its best. If you need help running your social media accounts, you could hire a freelancer (or a team of freelancers) with experience and skills in social media.

#5. Run a social media challenge

By making a social media challenge, you can make content that goes viral and boost your presence on social media. You can get attention on social media for your brand by making a fun and viral challenge and asking your followers to do something crazy. Make sure the social media challenge has something to do with your brand and is unique or stands out. Don't forget to make a hashtag that people can use to find their way back to your brand.

You can also turn your social media challenge into a contest to get more people interested in your brand. Give the winner a free service from your business. This will encourage people to take part in your challenge and share it with their followers, which will spread the word about what your business does.

6. Make plans to keep clients

Bring back customers to your business to automate it. Finding new clients takes a lot of time and work when you start your own business or work as a freelancer. Once you find these clients, you can make and use plans to keep them as clients. A retainer plan is a business strategy that makes sure you'll always have customers who come back and a steady flow of money. These programs include deals, package plans, and loyalty programs, all of which help you get to know your customers better.

1. Offer services that need to be renewed every so often

Make sure you stay in touch with your clients over time. You can offer a lot of services that require a long-term commitment or a regular renewal. Customers will need your services over and over again if you clean houses, teach a language, or walk dogs. Getting to know these clients and keeping in touch with them will not only help your business but also give you a steady source of income. For ongoing services, you can offer your customers a subscription or package deal. For example, if they buy 5 classes or dog walks in advance, they get a discount compared to paying for them one at a time.

2: Instead of quoting each new job separately, offer packages.

You can offer package deals for one-time services, just like you can give customers a discount if they pay for ongoing services ahead of time. Think about the service you already give your customers and pair it with similar services to give them a reason to pick you. If you have everything a customer needs, it's very easy for them to do business with you.

In addition to making things easier for your customers, you can create a package deal that either gives a discount or at least looks like a discount. This is possible because the services you offer are so valuable. If you are a freelance web designer or graphic designer, you know that your clients will need new marketing materials or a new website every three months. You can put together a package that includes a website design and updates, or you can put together a bundle of marketing materials. People will like how easy it is, and you'll be able to count on a steady stream of income.

3: Make customer loyalty programs

Loyalty programs are very popular for a reason, and that reason is that they work. When a business has a loyalty program, people are more likely to use it and come back. There are different kinds of loyalty programs, such as those based on points, tiers, and perks.

- Loyalty programs based on points: Customers get points for buying things, signing up to get emails, and giving feedback. When a customer gets a certain number of points, they'll be able to get something for free or get a discount.

- Loyalty programs with tiers. Depending on how much money a customer spends, they move up to a different tier. The higher the rank, the more money they spend. Each level has its own discounts, bonuses, and benefits. The higher the level, the better the benefit.

- Loyalty programs based on perks: Loyalty programs based on bonuses are usually smaller and involve free items that come with a purchase or service, often as a surprise. Think about free small samples of beauty products or free digital extras. Another example will be if you own a business that washes and cleans people's cars. As a bonus, you could wax the car or give it a free air freshener.

4. Do a survey

Ask your customers what they think of your services by giving them a survey. It gives you the chance to keep doing the things that people love about your business and improve the things that could use a little more work. Your customers will like that you are willing to hear what they have to say and will also like any changes you make based on what they say. This will also interest your customers and give you a chance to thank them for using your services and learn more about them. If you want to do a digital survey but don't have the skills, Fiverr has tools to help you do so.

5. Provide personalization

By making the experience more personal, you can attract more customers. RILA's (R)Tech Center for Innovation and Accenture say that 63 per cent of customers want a personalized brand experience. To do this, you need to find out what your customers want. Asking your customers when their birthday is and sending them a happy birthday message with a discount or coupon is a good way to start personalizing.

Some services let users send newsletters to their clients that include their names in the email greeting.

6. Don't forget to take care of your customers.

Customer service is a very important part of running a business and the best way to keep customers coming back to you for more business. It gives your business a personal touch that people will remember, just like the first step of personalization.

It's almost a given that a customer who is happy will come back. You can't guarantee that everyone will have a perfect experience with your service, even if that's what you want to do at first. Customer service is a great way to fix any problem your customers have. If a customer is unhappy with their first experience, they can let you know through your surveys or comments. You can then reach out to them and fix the problem.

Getting to know your customers on a real level. Talk directly to your customers through the social media sites they use. We've already talked about how to make a name for yourself on social media, and now you can use that to connect with your customers and potential customers. You can't just post and expect people to like it. You also need to interact with your customers' posts, especially if they share something about your product.

Post any good reviews that people leave about your services and be sure to thank them. If people post reviews that aren't very good, it's a great chance to get feedback from customers. Talk to them in private and see if there's anything you can do to make things better.

Providing great customer service is a work in progress. It's a good idea to make it a rule that you answer your customers' questions quickly. Taking the time to remember details about your customers and saying "please" and "thank you" goes a long way.

It's also important to be there for your customers when they need you, so you should offer support around the clock. No, we don't think you should go without sleep and always be available for your customers. You can make a chatbot that users can use to ask simple questions (or you have a Fiverr freelancer to create one for you). If the customer's question is too hard for the bot to answer, they can send it to a real customer service person or send it to your email.

Conclusion

The job market is tough, and many of us are stuck looking for work in an economy that isn't sure what will happen. Your best bet is to start a side business based on yourself and the skills you already have. With the steps we just went over, you can figure out what you're good at and use it to your advantage. Your skills will be the foundation of your business, and your business will be stronger if you create value for your customers, focus on marketing, and provide great customer service. By dividing your audience into groups and putting your attention on your customers, you can turn people who have a problem into loyal, repeat customers. In these uncertain times, a steady stream of income will come from attracting and keeping these customers.

CHAPTER 2

CREATIVE ENTREPRENEURSHIP - 3 STEPS TO TRANSFORM TALENT INTO SELF EMPLOYMENT CASH!

Now that everyone has access to a computer and the internet, anyone can succeed as a self-employed person. It's incredible how these instruments have transformed everything. How can you utilize these resources and the market to turn your talent into money? Although very easy to execute, it is not simple. For many people, switching from receiving a regular salary can be difficult. Many of us have been conditioned to believe that attending college or a trade school and finding employment are the only ways to earn a living. Additionally, we have been conditioned to think that the only thing that can offer "benefits," such as health insurance, is a job. However, more and more young people are leaving college and starting their businesses. They can pay a monthly premium for health insurance and benefit from an HSA (Health Savings Account), which is only available to self-employed people.

I want to establish what I mean by creative entrepreneurship before moving on. The technique of earning a living off of a skill or ability while employing modest resources and avoiding debt is known as creative entrepreneurship. Entrepreneurship with a creative flair is for regular folks. While it can be achievable for some, becoming a millionaire isn't necessarily the end. The objective is to successfully run your own business, earn a living doing what you enjoy, and possibly work from home or a tiny office. Creative entrepreneurship is not about investing in a franchise, hiring workers, and setting up shop. It is unnecessary to purchase numerous expensive newspaper advertisements, maintain a sizeable overhead, obtain bank financing, assemble a board of directors, go public, and issue shares. However, the result can be a liveable to six-figure income with a comfortable lifestyle and little expense, risk, or debt.

I've developed the phrase "creative entrepreneurialism" to characterize my way of life. My first company was one for which I had received training. I attended college and graduated with an advertising degree. Then I agreed to work as a freelance sales representative for promotional goods advertising. I eventually founded my own promotional goods business. Now, I've diversified into different fields aligned with my passions, experiences, and knowledge. The highest level of capitalist freedom is provided by creative entrepreneurship. With just a laptop, phone, and website, we may work from home and support ourselves by doing what we love or are good at.

I've listed three stages below to help you start your creative entrepreneurship path.

These are the fundamental actions you must take to begin a career as a self-employed person. Give yourself 1-3 years to implement these changes. Try to work part-time at both your current job and your own business. Although relatively straightforward, this technique is not. The goal of creative entrepreneurship is not to take out loans but rather to develop a clientele and use the money you earn from them to invest in expanding your company as it succeeds. Because you are your own boss, you will need to develop new ways of thinking, set your own objectives, develop your own vision for your business, and plan your own vacations and days off.

Purchase Some Tools:

1. Get a laptop, printer, toll-free number, cell phone, and workspace by making an investment.

2. Make sure your laptop has a reliable art application like Corel Draw or Microsoft Publisher.

3. Ensure that the workspace is a tidy, uncluttered section of your house, garage, or apartment.

4. Keep your living space and workspace distinct.

I started in a basement and finished my shift when I went upstairs to go home. Utilize your tools properly. While you are still earning a regular salary, you are allowed to do this on the weekends and in the evenings.

• Acquire Some Knowledge: Discover your passion and a practical marketing strategy for it. Dana Beasley, a digital portrait artist for Pet City customers, is passionate about art and animals. She is not a fine artist. Create a website business selling sentimental CDs if, for example, you love music but are aware that you won't be a rock star. You must enrol in graphic design, website design, sales, and bookkeeping courses. Many of these courses can be completed online or with software tutorials. These fundamentals will help you manage your career as a self-employed person. Improve your skills in your area of expertise. Earn your CPA if you are a bookkeeper; if you are an architect, get your license as an architect. Get training or certifications in whatever you enjoy doing or are skilled at.

- Start Getting Clients: It's time to begin acquiring clients. When you initially start out, it could be a good idea to work for nothing while you are still employed at your job that generates income. In exchange for a written endorsement of how fantastic your company's product or service is, ask a friend or member of your family to let you practice on them. Your clientele will increase as you gain experience, knowledge, and credibility if you incorporate this into your marketing materials and website. Your graphic design knowledge will be useful when creating the marketing materials you need to draw in customers. To assist you in creating your logo, business cards, and letterhead, you can also contract a graphic designer on a project-by-project basis. As you get more clients, you should always invest a portion of your income in more sophisticated marketing initiatives to boost and expand the business, such as branding with promotional merchandise, email consultations, newsletters, and postcards.

Owning your firm necessitates personal growth because it can only expand to what you do. To get you to complete independence, you'll need ongoing training and guidance. As your creative juices start to flow once more, you can extend to other businesses after you attain independence in one. Making a living doing what you are good at and love is the highest kind of freedom and joy. You may significantly contribute to yourself, your family, society, and the world around you by engaging in creative entrepreneurship!

How to Turn Talents Into Strengths

Generalizations exist as a shortcut to presenting what is considered a universal reality. They can, however, rise to misconceptions, one of which is that older people are less adept at technology, mainly social media.

There is a connection between this and employability. Put age aside and consider the following circumstances of people:

What if...you're looking for work, and one of the job requirements is digital literacy?

What if...you are employed, and your company demands a significant improvement in performance that requires you to work in novel ways?

What if...you wish to change jobs or careers and discover that what has previously served you well is no longer sufficient to enable you to take the next step?

Back to the options. Consider yourself at the centre of a circular room with seven doorways. A way can be found on the opposite side of each door. You have no idea where they might lead. Imagine one of those doors is red, and behind it is the route that makes you feel most at home, allows you to be your best, and ignites your passion. How do you open the red door? Don't forget that you may go through a pink door (or any other colour!) to get to your red door. Walking through a green door may be too much of a reach or simply not for you. It's all about trying new things and finding your ideal match.

Using social media as an example, here's how you may adopt a positive attitude toward change (and walk through the red door) by recognizing and developing your talents:

"Although I don't use social media, I have attended many business events, have enjoyed them, and have brought back some good practices and contacts for others to explore."

TIP 1: Find out what works well and expand on it (the best of what is). "I have identified that my competence in our work sector, the breadth of my experience, and my pleasant character enable me to work well at these events."

TIP 2: Identify what elements enable you to operate well and what may be repeated (why is it working?)

"I've envisaged a scenario where I could do some of these things online. Although it will test me, I can picture myself demonstrating my knowledge, publishing testimonials, emphasizing relevant experience in various profiles, and yet meeting people in person through the relationships I make."

TIP 3: Create a vision of what you're doing that will lead to its success. How would it appear? "I chatted with a few friends and coworkers to tease out some of my assumptions and gain their viewpoint and thoughts."

TIP 4: Establish a dialogue that allows for an honest and open inquiry into all aspects of the vision (let's test my assumptions). "It is now evident who can assist me and how I can make this happen."

TIP 5: Identify the present aspects of your strengths that can be used to develop the vision. What do I support? (What ought to be) " "I've devised a strategy for what I'm going to do and when I will accomplish it. I'll know when I've accomplished it and what constitutes success."

TIP 6: Create an action plan that leverages the leverage points revealed in these characteristics of your strengths to create and deliver the vision (what will be).

Even imagined success might provide a sense of accomplishment. It might sometimes feel more liberated and encouraging to start with the good. Remember that your attitude is still a decision with both positive and negative effects. Finding and unlocking your red door will feel free rather than terrifying.

CHAPTER 3

HAVE A WINNING MENTALITY WHILE CONVERTING YOUR SKILLS INTO A LUCRATIVE CAREER OR BUSINESS.

Working in a field that interests you may be a pleasurable and profitable endeavour for anyone of any age. However, the excitement will soon fade if your business fails to make a profit quickly. Naturally, there are some businesses, such as affiliate sales, where your gain will be postponed until the commission payout cycle occurs.

Profits in such an enterprise typically don't materialize as quickly as they would in, say, the sale of digitally created works.

Making money is the ultimate goal of any enterprise. Profits at the end of the fiscal year are directly correlated to the health of a business.

In the early phases of a firm, it may be necessary to invest more money than the company brings in. Nonetheless, losing money while in operation is unacceptable and must be stopped immediately. Collecting debts can be disastrous.

Your firm will be more secure when you keep costs under control, seize genuine opportunities, take measured risks, and have a plan to generate consistent revenue. You'll need money to invest in options and a collection of marketing tools to make the most of them.

Many startups fail because they can't afford to keep going. It's impossible to bring a concept to fruition without first soliciting financial support from others.

First, you must ensure that your product, service, or idea is novel; second, there is a market for it; and third, it is within your area of competence.

To be successful, your company must provide clients with something of genuine and unique value. If you go above and beyond what your clients anticipate and your rivals do, your business will thrive. Improve your offering by including a function that competitors lack.

In today's competitive marketplace, excellence is no longer rewarded. You need to step up your performance. You must outperform the competition. And it would help if you outdid your previous efforts.

In what ways can this be possible? You can better serve both as you learn more about your business and your customers. Profits should be reinvested in purchasing cutting-edge equipment, training in advanced methods, and the ongoing enhancement of product quality. If you follow these guidelines, you can expect to retain your loyal consumers for the long haul. Business success requires a combination of savvy marketing, product presentation, decision making, problem-solving, and dogged persistence to reach one's goals. Possessing confidence in one's organizational skills and commercial acumen is also essential.

Your goal should be to reduce the possibility of failure while increasing the likelihood of success. Achieving this goal will be easier if you work on improving the abilities above.

Keep financial success in mind as a top priority in making a company decision.

If you run your business with the maturity and dependability of an adult, you can quickly amass a substantial fortune. Maximize your company's earnings at all costs. When you can make a dollar, you shouldn't take a dime. By anticipating long stretches with lower income due to factors outside your control, you can better manage them if and when they occur.

If you take the mentality of always looking for the bright side of things, you'll bring in many new customers and a lot of money. Remember that making money is the ultimate objective of any company venture.

Five attributes you need to master to succeed in business

The business world is changing, so we need to change along with it. But we don't want to respond to a changing world; we want to shape it and be ahead of the pack. Here are five skills you'll need to learn if you want to adapt to this new world, do well in it, and stand out.

1. Think critically.

Critical thinking is when you question assumptions, claims, and points of view instead of just taking them at face value, like when you say, "A Harvard professor said it online, so it must be true." It's a vital part of making wise choices. And that, in turn, is the key to doing well at almost anything.

People seem to have forgotten how to think logically, though, as of late. With so much information and sound bites coming at us all the time, it's more important than ever to be able to question what's real and what's not, to think logically and not generalize from a single piece of information, and to understand how things work.

So, question everything, especially what everyone else says. Listen to people who examine your own beliefs and the beliefs of most people. Don't give in to the urge to see things as black and white or "us vs them." Learn to look at the world from different angles, points of view, and points of view.

2. Focus and self-control.

We are way past the point of too much information and communication. Even hard-working people who should know better sit down to work and find that after a few tweets, texts, and emails, half the day is gone, and all the work is still there.

Focus and discipline have always been essential for success in almost any field, but these days, even the most disciplined people find it harder to avoid being distracted. And it doesn't look like that will change any time soon.

Now, more than ever, you need to learn how to block out the noise without what's important. That is not simple. But you can't get things done if you're too distracted and lack the discipline to pay attention to what's most important. And if you can't do something, someone else will.

3. Being human.

Authentically, we are becoming digital copies of who we are in the real world. That would be fine if our personas were the same as who we are. Instead, avatars are carefully made based on social norms, popular themes, and people's hopes. We sort the information we share. We act more and more like living sound bites—virtual actors playing cardboard characters in a flat digital world.

But honest communication and authentic relationships are what make a business work. To run a business, you must get investors to give you money, customers to buy your products, and employees to work hard for you. Ultimately, a person is on both ends of every business deal. People who try to be different online will have a significant advantage in a world where everyone looks the same. Have the courage to be yourself instead of hiding behind your social media avatar and personal brand. Put away your social network and start making friends in real life. Listen to what other people say and go with your gut. That's the only way to connect with, get to know, and understand other people. Be human.

4. Doing what needs to be done.

It's a myth that most successful business leaders are driven by high ideals and goals that are too high. None of the successful executives I've known got where they are by walking around with their heads in the clouds. They got there by working hard and putting one foot before the other.

Entrepreneurs who do well can bring people together and get them to work toward a common goal. They have a strong sense of responsibility, accountability, and work ethic. They are born to figure out how to fix problems. And problems, obstacles, and risks don't stop them—instead, they give them energy.

They also know what their goals and top priorities are. They know what they want to do and do it. No matter what, they deliver what they promise, get the job done, and meet the needs of those who depend on them.

A reader recently laughed at one of my columns about what makes startups successful. He said that all you need are ideas. Everyone has opinions, which is the problem. What we need are people who take action and are driven to get things done. This is a skill that will become more valuable as time goes on.

5. The desire to win.

Ecommerce and the growth of the global economy have made it easier for businesses to compete with each other. As technology lowers the barriers to entry and more and more companies move into each other's markets, there are new competitors everywhere. At the same time, we are putting less emphasis on competition and individual success in our schools. As we make everything the same, people lose their desire to compete and win. We're starting to think that competition is bad.

That makes for an interesting contrast, or, if you will, a competition gap. There's no doubt that the situation is both a challenge and an opportunity. On the one hand, there is a lot of competition. Things are hard out there. On the other hand, most young people entering the workforce have a disadvantage if they are not very driven to compete and win. This gap will only get bigger as time goes on.

Markets are basically zero-sum games, which means that there is a limited amount of market share. And even though markets are elastic—they grow over time—at a macro level, there is usually one winner and more than one loser in every business transaction. One business only gets the job. Only one company is chosen to do what needs to be done. In the real world, you're always in a way competing with other people.

But that doesn't make it something bad.

It's a good thing when one product, company, or candidate beats out another based on its own strengths. It's also not a shame to lose. This is how we learn to do better the next time.

Competition is how new technologies replace old ones, how small companies grow into big ones, and how good performers become great ones.

The point is that many great companies, if not most of them, are started and run by fierce competitors. Google went after Apple hard when it came to making smartphones. Travis Kalanick gets a lot of flak for being so competitive, but in just five years, he has built Uber into a $41 billion company.

Competitive spirit, or the constant desire to win, is a key to success that will only become more important as the gap between you and the competition grows. You can learn to change and improve these skills by doing them. And that will give you a long-term edge in a world that is always changing.

CHAPTER 4

TO TURN IDEAS INTO MONEY, ONE MUST THINK LIKE AN ENTREPRENEUR AND TAKE MENTAL SAFETY PRECAUTIONS.

Build walls like Babylon

To continue concentrating on your goal, you must silence all the distractions around you. If you want to be able to think and dream large constantly, you need to be conscious of the negative voices surrounding you and be prepared to block them out. Let's pretend you've done the work necessary to figure out what it is that you want, what it is that you desire.

You have decided to work hard toward accomplishing it. You start imagining it already taking place, and then you take the initial steps toward really making it happen. You are astounded by how you feel about it and get a newfound sense of vitality from it. Making a choice can accomplish this goal. When you make a good choice, scientific research indicates that certain chemicals are released in the brain, which contributes to the sense of joy that follows. You have promised yourself that you will follow through with your plans this time. You can keep saying this throughout the day as you ask yourself, "what took me so long to see the end outcome as clearly as I do today!?" your excitement increases. Wow! Exhilarating is one word to describe the sensation!

Then, CRASH! When you tell a buddy about your decision the following day, they don't seem too excited about it, and their disinterest is as palpable as the fog in London. You pick up on the disdain in their tone, and without even recognizing what is happening, you let their apathy and condescension pull you back into their world of mediocrity.

The rise in serotonin from the previous day gradually fades away and returns to its baseline level, which is the chemical equivalent of depression. Comparable to how easily one could puncture the taut side of a latex balloon with a pin. It's finished. You let folly drain your momentum. Your aspiration was thwarted by the criticism of a person who does not believe.

The issue here is not that you brought up the concept before you had a well-defined plan, nor is your friend even manifestly less capable of abstract thought than you are. The issue originates from within yourself. If you continue to allow this to occur, it is clear that you are not prepared to take the steps necessary to become a successful entrepreneur or solopreneur. You will never make it to your destination!

You have to be able to construct a barrier around the location that you see in your dreams before you can visit it. In the same way that the city of Babylon fortified itself against hostile invaders by erecting a higher and thick wall than anybody could have imagined... On the other hand, you need to use the same approach with your frame of mind. Guard it as if it were the most prosperous country in the entire world. The bigger you think an issue is, the more thoroughly you need to investigate it. People who don't get the concept of "thinking large" will always exist.

There will always be people who try to sell you their satire. Be conscious of it, anticipate their arrival, and get ready to put up a defence against them as soon as they show up. Whenever I hear that, I can't help but smile. Don't bother defending yourself or trying to compete with their ways of doing things. Don't throw away your hard work!

However, some of the best things to do are the following: spend most of your time maintaining the flow of rhythm with your ideas.

o   Surround yourself with people who share your values and can provide guidance that will assist you in achieving your goals; always be on the lookout for such people, and have faith that you will find them. It is incredible how many resources, in the shape of people and relationships, will present themselves to you once your wall has been constructed and your course has been established.

o,   Keep reading books and stories that inspire you and propel you forward when you can't go it alone...you can collect an enormous amount of ideas and inspiration from book series like Chicken Soup for the Entrepreneur's Soul or other success stories.

o   Good advice comes in many forms, so collect all varieties of it. The Internet, acquaintances, wisdom from our past leaders, friends... o Keep reading books and stories that inspire you and propel you forward when you can't go it alone.

Turning Time Into Money - What You Need To Do Now

You have probably come across the expression "time is money" on more than one occasion. However, the question that needs to be answered is how one may apply tactics for time management to turn time into money.

You will be able to connect to this if you are employed by someone else and do not have complete control over how you spend your time.

You can relate to this situation if you are self-employed and operate at your own pace. Still, you are constantly under pressure to meet deadlines and other significant deliverables established by your stakeholders and the demands of your consumers.

Those who are content with their work and manage to perform it successfully over time will experience the tremendous success. The waste of time and the bad habit of procrastination is, in all likelihood, going to be the most significant obstacles on the path to professional achievement. To successfully overcome these obstacles, you need to start each day's work with a well-defined plan for how you will manage your time. You can do so if you:

PRIORITIZE

In addition to increasing your potential income, cultivating the talent of "smart prioritization" allows you to see outcomes in a more timely manner. Make sure that, before you begin your day in the traditional sense, you have made a list of everything that needs to be done and a rough estimate of how much time will be required to finish each of those activities. You have to get this done right away at the beginning of your work day since it will help you gain a better grasp of the chores that are still waiting for you; as a result, it will give you a better notion of how well you are progressing toward your goals. Along with compiling the list of things that need to be done, you will also need to prioritize the activities on the list. Longterm projects and time-consuming undertakings that may still be pursued the following day should be placed at the bottom of your list. Urgent deliverables and those offering more significant cash returns should be placed on your list. Focus on the activities that will most likely result in monetary gain for either the firm you currently work for or the enterprise you run on your own. Why? Because if you continuously follow this strategy, you will build an operating reserve of cash, which your employer or bank account will appreciate if you are the business owner. This cash will be in your bank account if you are the business owner.

SCHEDULE

In addition to exercising "smart prioritization," "wise scheduling" is another essential skill for effective time management that will assist you in increasing your work productivity and financial cash flow. To put it briefly, if you plan your day effectively, you will accomplish more. When you plan your phone calls, attend meetings, engage in marketing activities, check your email, and complete all of the other mundane things in an ordered method daily, you will begin to see an increase in your earnings. As long as your schedule and the amount of work you have to do allow for it, you will be able to pursue many tasks at the same time successfully.

It would help if you also thought about switching the activities that you consider fun with those that you find boring. Your level of enjoyment will be lower, and you will get less work done if you start the day by focusing on activities that you do not find delightful. Because of this, you need to combine different activities, as this will ensure that you feel successful, not only for the enjoyable ones but also for the ones you first detested doing. You are turning all your time into gold by continually applying this strategy throughout the day, even though some of those hours were not particularly pleasurable for you.

In addition, you need to make sure that you stick to the tasks on your to-do list and your work schedule. Managing your time well means that there will be instances in which you will need to perform task 3 before task 2, rather than the other way around because it will fit your planned timetable a lot better. Being flexible can help you achieve more extraordinary achievements since you should tailor your work to the requirements of the current situation rather than relying solely on the plan you devised the day before.

A computerized time management system should be considered if you are employed in a setting with a significant amount of work and multiple teams. They assist you in saving a considerable amount of time and effort, which you would have otherwise spent manually scheduling your workday. Because of the time you save each day at work, you will be able to take on additional responsibilities, ultimately leading to increased earnings. This will enable you to convert your valuable time into financial gain.

YOU SHOULD MAKE THE MOST OF YOUR FREE TIME

You will occasionally find that you have some time to yourself. Be sure to put some of your downtimes into getting yourself ready for the times when you'll have more on your plate. When it comes to managing your time effectively, being proactive and having the ability to predict upcoming duties will always pay off. Therefore, rather than spending your spare time chitchatting with your coworkers, you can put that time to better use by making plans for the impending responsibilities you have. The everyday duties of filing documents and organizing critical paperwork that may clutter the desk if stacked up for a while can be properly completed by office workers in their leisure time, which can be used to effectively utilize their spare time. This can be used by people who are self-employed to make a phone call and negotiate a discount of $100 per month on their business telephone bill. After you have finished saving 1,200 dollars annually by spending 27 minutes on the phone, you can then go about your business and enjoy the time that is left over for you.

CHAPTER 5

HOW TO BRING BUSINESS SKILLS TO THE INTERNET MARKETPLACE: KNOW YOUR COMPETITION

Analyzing the competition is one of the first steps in beginning any business. Knowing how to place a company in the market, who to target, what prices to set, and who to keep an eye on are all critical decisions that any business owner is aware of. The online market is similar in this regard.

However, when a company decides to "go online," this understanding rarely gets translated. Perhaps the initial setup is so overwhelming that little consideration is given to anything outside a website's design and content. However, despite its rapid expansion, the internet remains a market. These same commercial acumens are also required in this situation.

You must first think like a search engine to understand what your competitors are doing well to succeed. By copying well-known keywords and phrases, you can gain traffic that would otherwise be sent to your competitors' websites.

In what is referred to as "Meta Tags," keywords are included. These tags include descriptions, titles, and keywords in the source code at the top of a webpage. In addition to content, search engines use this data to rank your website for various search terms. Choose "View" and

"Source" from the toolbar to view the source of any website to access this data.

Don't lose hope if you think this code looks like some strange alien language after looking at it. Numerous applications can search rivals' websites for this data and offer a comprehensive report in plain English. You will be inundated with products if you search for anything about search engine optimization (SEO), one of the newest hot subjects. The risk is to get into too much hype and avoid paying for promises since search engines are not as susceptible to deception as we are.

Links are another essential component. The search engines will rank your page favourably if they believe it to be an authority on a particular topic. Similar to votes, when someone links to your website, they are essentially "voting" in favour of it. Beware of "link farms" (pages made exclusively of links), as these will not boost your site's positioning because the weight of this vote is determined by how many other websites they connect to. Although visitors might not visit your site directly through these connections, they will help with overall search engine positioning. The most straightforward approach to acquiring links is through internet directories.

To get back to the competition, you can use a link popularity checker online to find out who is linking to other websites. You might try to get these websites to link back to you in this way. Always remember that targeted traffic is preferable; therefore, seek out links from websites that have material that is similar to yours. It should go without saying that if your company sells stamps, the most okay links will come from websites dedicated to collecting them.

Time Management Skills for Business Owners

As a business owner, you know that if you want to be productive, you need to manage your time well to have a good balance between work and your personal life. Every part of your life takes time and effort, so you likely often wonder how to balance the time you spend growing your business with the time you spend living your life. Even though your personal life is essential to your health, if you want your business to do well, you need to give it the time and energy it needs.

Follow these five tips for better time management, and you'll be a more productive business owner.

1) Use technology to your benefit.

It can be hard and helpful to run a business in the digital age. How you use the technology you have will determine the answer. Since social networking is both a popular business tool and a social asset, it can be hard to use it to get work done without wasting time. You have to learn to control yourself. Use your phone and other gadgets wisely, and don't waste time on Twitter and Facebook.

2) Multitasking gets too much credit

With things like laptops and smartphones that are easy to take with you, you are probably tempted to do as much work as possible in a single day. If you're the parent who watches your daughter's soccer game with one eye on your work and the other on your laptop while sitting in the stands, do everyone a favour and leave the computer at home. Remember that there won't be any money-making activities on the little league soccer field. Your family and your business need your full attention, so set aside time for each and try not to let the two times clash.

3) Plan for emergencies.

Life doesn't always go as planned, so it's essential to be ready for surprises. Set aside time in your day when you have nothing to do in case something comes up immediately. If everything goes well, who knows? You might be able to use that extra time to relax for a while. That sounds good.

4) There was a reason why "Do Not Disturb" signs were made.

As a business owner, you try to be there for your employees and customers whenever they need you. You have been taught that this is a good business move. But how can you get anything done when you're constantly putting everyone else's needs before your own? When you have work to do for a long time, don't be afraid to put up that "Do Not Disturb" sign and get things done. This can also work for people who run a business from home but don't use it too much.

When you work from home, people often come in and ask for things.

5) Plans are meant to be kept.

How often do you set up a meeting and then let it last longer than the time you set aside for it? There are no appointments that are so great that you should do this every time. When you set a time and date for an appointment, try as hard as you can to keep that time slot. Your time doesn't come cheap, so don't waste it on meetings, conversations, and activities that don't get you anywhere.

CHAPTER 6

HERE ARE THE TOP 10 REQUIREMENTS FOR BUSINESS SUCCESS (AND IN LIFE)

HERE YOU WILL FIND ACCOUNTS OF THE LIVES OF SEVERAL PROSPEROUS BUSINESSPEOPLE WHO HAVE ALSO ACHIEVED PERSONAL SUCCESS.

There are a lot of books about how to be successful in business, and there are also a lot of books about how to be successful in life. You can find another thousand articles about the subject on the web, and tomorrow, another thousand will be written. Because happiness is such a broad topic and depends on so many different things, it can be hard to boil it down to a shortlist that anyone can read and use in their own lives.

But some common themes run through all of those thousands of books and articles, as well as the countless legends and stories. You'll find human principles that many of us think about but don't try hard enough to reach. You'll hear about goals and decisions that we all wish we could reach but often don't understand. Here are ten things that people who have been successful in business (and in life) tend to have. How many of these do you already have, and how many do you need to get?

1. Don't be afraid

Do you want to know why people think being successful in business is such a hard thing to do? Even though there are obvious problems to be solved, one of the biggest problems is getting over the fear of starting a business. Most people spend all day at their boring day jobs thinking about how they could start a business that does well. They never leave the security of a pay-check because they are too afraid of the unknown that comes with starting a business. If you want to stand out from that group, you need to figure out how to deal with your own fears. Don't feel bad; you're not the only one. When I quit my job to start my own business, I was making twice as much money outside of work as I was at my eight-hour job. I was still very afraid of failing.

But if you want to be truly successful in business, this is just the beginning of your journey. Overcoming your fears and getting started is a good thing, but the real tests of a fearless entrepreneur will happen all the time, like starting a conversation at a networking mixer, asking for the sale on a big deal, cutting ties with a partner who is hurting the business, and perhaps the scariest of all, watching a business fail (Henry Ford's businesses failed twice before he came up with his famous assembly line). A person who can fail horribly but isn't afraid to get back up and try again and again until they succeed is truly fearless.

2. Understand Finance

People talk all the time about how a well-known business started in someone's basement or garage. In fact, they talk about it so much that it's become a romantic idea that going from nothing to something is what makes a true entrepreneur. Most successful business ideas couldn't be more different from the truth: if you want to make it, you'll need money. But that doesn't mean you have to have a lot of money when you're just starting out. What's more important is knowing how money works and how to use it in the best way to make it grow.

Robert Kiyosaki is best known for teaching the world how important financial literacy is for entrepreneurs. People who live from pay-check to pay-check are also likely to have a lot of things that cost them money, like car and house payments, credit cards, and other material things. Those who know about money, on the other hand, know how important it is to build assets, which are things that make them money. Once your asset column starts to grow, you can learn how to invest even more money. To be a successful business owner, you must know how to put your money to work.

3. Become a better leader

When you face your fears and start a business, you've taken the first step toward becoming a leader. As we'll talk about soon, a big part of your ultimate success will depend on how well you help others find their own. Many of us look up to successful business people like football fans look up to a star quarterback or wide receiver. But it's always the team that these people lead that makes them successful in the end. You have to learn to lead on some level if you want other people to join you in your business, believe what you say, or pay you money for a product or service you offer.

Even though you need to have leadership skills to be successful in business, that doesn't mean you have to be the CEO, face of the company, or person "in charge." When Google started to really grow, its' founders, who were engineers and not CEOs, hired a successful CEO, Eric Schmidt, to run the company. Sometimes, being able to lead a group or a team comes down to having the right charisma and message to get the right people to do what needs to be done for the whole thing to work. A great soldier might be good at leading troops on the field but not running the entire war. A great product designer might also be bad at selling. But a good leader will find out what people are good at and where they are weak. They will also know who to put where to ensure their company is a real success.

4. Use Your Leverage

One of the biggest obstacles that will keep an entrepreneur from getting what they want is not knowing what to do with the opportunities that come their way. This is why leverage is such an important business concept, and it takes a certain kind of mind to think "outside the box" to find value in a new relationship or situation. People who are afraid to quit their day jobs are also the same people who don't know how to make the most of their assets and relationships. On the other hand, a successful entrepreneur is always looking for ways to make money and find new opportunities every day.

When life gives you lemons, make lemonade, as the old saying goes. This is a great way to move your business forward. Many people will make and drink their own lemonade. A real entrepreneur will make lemonade and sell it to people who don't have any lemons. They will use the money they make to buy more lemons or start a new business. Even though Donald Trump is a controversial politician now, he is a great example of an entrepreneur who used leverage to buy important pieces of real estate or make very profitable business deals over and over again. Whether you like him or dislike him, his book The Art of the Deal is a great way to learn about how leverage can help someone become a huge success.

5. Acquire Partners

We've already talked about how being a leader is one of the most important skills to "move the chains" in business. For a leader to be great, he or she must have a group of people who believe in the mission and want to move forward. That's why putting together a great team of partners is such an important part of any business that makes money. Many people start out alone and wear many hats, but a business can only grow so far if there is only one source of energy, inspiration, and the actual sweat equity it takes to keep the lights on.

As we learn more about what it means to be successful in business and in life, we'll see that a true "business owner" doesn't have to be involved in the day-to-day operations for the business to run and make money. The classic book "The E-Myth" tells a great story about how many people try to run a business on their own and fail. Instead, you should use your leadership skills to encourage other people to use their own skills as part of a team for the good of the company as a whole. This doesn't just mean hiring the right people; it also means knowing who to shake hands with, making strategic partnerships, and using the leverage we discussed earlier to get other people interested in your business. When you reach a certain level of success, it will feel even better to share it with everyone who helped make it happen.

6. Being in the right frame of mind

So far, we've talked about some of the essential ideas you need to know to be successful in business. But how do you define real success? Is it money, sales, or the effect of what you do on the world around you? In the end, business success only matters if it leads to life success, and the first step is having the right attitude about it. No one cares about rich people who hate the world in which they live. Everyone knows the story of Ebenezer Scrooge, the bitter older man who had a lot of money but did nothing but make other people's lives complicated.

To live a happy and fulfilling life, you need to know what's important and build your values around what you can do daily to bring that world into being. Sure, a lot of people who start a business want to be able to take care of themselves financially. But what do you do with all that money when you finally get it? People who think that having money means being able to buy more "things" to make themselves feel better than other people will never be successful. Entrepreneurs who focus on how they can make money to help others and solve problems have the right mindset to be truly happy and be seen in a positive light by their peers and partners. They are the true definition of the word "success."

7. Being Thankful

Every day, our world changes at a speed that any of us can understand. In the last 30 to 50 years, technology has changed how we talk to our neighbours and loved ones and how we talk to people we do business with around the world. People who have grown up with this technology often take it for granted, never stopping to "smell the roses" and realize that they live in a fantastic time in history and that they should be very thankful for everything they have, from the electricity that powers their lights to the cars that get them to their next meeting to the smartphones in their pockets.

People who are thankful for the world they live in are happy in business and life. These people thank the barista for their coffee in the morning, hold the door open for others, and pay attention to the people they are talking to. Successful entrepreneurs should never forget the people, places, and things that helped them get from their humble beginnings to where they are now.

When you're next on a plane, think about how funny it is that Louis CK said you're "sitting in a chair in the sky," and be thankful for all the great things we do daily.

8. How to stay healthy

Your money and success won't help you if you're not around to using them, so why would you live in such a way that puts your health at risk? What good is being excited about your business dreams if you won't be there to see them come true? Too many of us get so caught up in the game of life that we never think about the damage we do to our bodies along the way. As business owners, our days are so busy with work and juggling projects that lunch breaks are just short breaks where we eat fast food to eliminate hunger. I eat with my mouth open.

Our nights turn into times when we sometimes work until we drop and use the stress of the day as an excuse to drink or do drugs to feel better. Is that how we measure success in life if we worship famous people who died too soon? Our love of money and things makes us greedy and uncertain about who we are and how others see us. We can never really be successful if we don't take care of our health. A leader needs to be strong, and we're not just talking about having a lean body or a lot of muscles. Your mind must also be in good shape to keep going through the day, get what you want, and enjoy it.

9. Making and Keeping Friends

We've talked about how important it is not to go alone when building your business; the same is true for your success and happiness. What's the point of doing anything if you don't have special people to share it with? No one wants to be the Bruce Wayne of their city, the fool with a big dining room table but no one to eat with.

People are naturally social, and having friends outside of work is essential. Your friends are people you can talk to about your life and who will be there to give you a high-five when you succeed and pick you up when you fail. Make sure they have the same attitude as you, show you gratitude, and continue to be a good influence in your life. Those who thrive on lousy energy are the ones you can use to bring the whole house down.

10. Why family is important

We've discussed why people become entrepreneurs and how important it is to know what goals they want to reach. Most people will start on their journey with money or power on their minds. Most of the time, these things are personal and done for one's benefit. However, someone who wants to be genuinely successful will do these things not just to share with their friends but, more importantly, with their families.

Not everyone has a great childhood, and you shouldn't have to share your money with your siblings just because you are related. Not every business owner has a soulmate, and not everyone will have kids. But it's essential to think about success in more ways than just the money or power it might bring. Real success comes from having a positive effect on your family and the people who will remember you and, hopefully, carry on what you started.

Use Your Business Skills Properly

Every entrepreneur's first goal should be to improve their business skills and strategies. There is a lot of training for business skills online, like "How to develop business skills" and "Learn business skills," but these materials are useless if you don't know how important business skills are. We have to see the big picture when it comes to business skills and work on getting better.

Here are some things you should think about if you want to start your own business.

Choose a way to go.

Elaine Pofeldt, a business journalist and the author of The Million Dollar, One-Person Business, says that you should think about what you're good at and not let uncertainty make you doubt your worth. She also says that you should say that if your goal is to leave your current job and start something new. You can use the skills you've learned throughout your career in a different field.

Most of the time, small business owners depend on their skills. The Kabbage lending platform surveyed in 2019 found that 82% of successful people were sure they had the skills and experience to run a business.

Sometimes, you may want to go in a completely different direction for the next level. In 2010, Faith McKinney, who is now 54, did that. She was a postal service janitor when she decided to work on her wish list, she says. She joined a networking group, and when the group's leader moved, she took the lead herself.

She found a teacher who helped her become a better speaker. And McKinney had a hard time until he met a cameraman for a local web magazine who needed on-air talent and gave him a chance. She worked hard to improve her skills and wasn't afraid to try new things, so now she works part-time as a TV producer in Indianapolis. McKinney didn't want to leave her job, but she loved her small side business.

Look at the environment.

Pofeldt says that once you have chosen a direction, you should look into how your skills can fill a need in the market. Think about what makes your company unique.

Please find out about possible competitors and their prices. She says the fastest way to figure out how much to charge is to ask people in the same line of work as you.

Heller says that it's essential to get feedback on what you're offering. This could mean talking to a mentor or coworkers to discover your strengths.

When making a product, sometimes the process is as easy as if people were testing it. Heller's friend started the vegan deli Unreal Deli, which makes cured meat, after making it for her husband, who eats meat.

She gave it to people she didn't know to try because he liked it. Her answers gave her the courage to talk to the deli's owners. Soon, people were asking her to make some of the enormous sandwiches in the area.

Why? She was willing to take a chance and let them know about the product. Heller says that in the end, the founder of Unreal Deli applied for a job on Shark Tank and got an investment from Mark Cuban, who turned his business into a multimillion-dollar business in six months.

Try to find help

Pofeldt says that to be successful, you must work hard and keep going. But you can go to a lot of places to get help. There are also a lot of free and cheap resources that can help you research the market, make a business plan, and find a mentor.

CHAPTER 7

BUILDING STRONG BUSINESS RELATIONSHIPS WILL HELP YOU BUILD BUSINESS SUCCESS.

The difference between commercial success and failure often comes down to the quality of the relationships a company maintains with its customers and the other companies it networks with. Without the assistance of other people, firms, and customers, your company's success is impossible. Building and maintaining healthy connections are required to achieve this goal. Building stronger relationships with others are one of the seven things you can do to improve your chances of commercial success.

1. Building lasting professional connections requires engaging in networking activities. Your network of contacts is the most critical asset of your company. Maintain consistent communication with your current and potential clients, vendors, business partners, coworkers, independent contractors, and acquaintances. You can network on a personal level or join one of the many groups that focus on networking. All dealings and conversations are not always required to be limited to business-related topics. Your firm will benefit more from your genuine efforts to pursue and nurture a relationship than from any form of impersonal advertising that you may do.

2.   Your identification can be found on your business card. Make sure to hand your clients and other contacts your business card when out networking. Your business card should have a professional appearance and include all your contact information, such as your telephone number, fax number, email address, and website address. Exchanging business cards is the first step in developing a professional relationship. Always keep your card on you, especially when you go to social occasions, and be ready to hand it out when the time is right based on the flow of the discussion.

Always make sure to swap business cards when the situation calls for it. If possible, write a personal message to yourself on the reverse of the business card about the person, the place where you met, and any questions the contact may have about your company. When you collect a card from a new connection, make sure to follow up with them within a week. A corporate executive who is actively engaged in networking will keep a database containing a collection of business cards as well as contact information.

3.   Use email for uncomplicated communication. Email is a very user-friendly and lowcost method of connecting with the people in your contact list. Even if there isn't currently a project in progress, you should nevertheless send regular emails to your clients. This makes it easier for other people to remember your company and the skills you offer long after you have finished a job.

You may send an informative letter to your customers about trends in the market, or you could introduce a brand-new product or service that your company is now providing. After you have established contact, it is appropriate to send a short email to your new contact expressing gratitude for the time they spent talking with you and expanding on your company's services.

Sending out messages via email is a powerful method of viral marketing. Your customers and other business contacts will pass along your message to others who might be interested in your work.

4. Ensure that your website has a polished and professional appearance. Your company's website needs to provide understandable information about your company and navigational instructions that are simple to grasp. On your website, your customers ought to have an easy time navigating different pages and locating content pertinent to their needs. You may optimize and boost the number of visitors to your website by optimizing it with popular search terms. Maintain a steady stream of up-to-date content on your website while removing anything that's become irrelevant or out-of-date.

You can go so far as to develop a forum for the industry linked to your website to stimulate online networking among professionals working in the field. This encourages consumers to continue visiting your website and helps to position your business as the industry leader in the relevant subject. You will also have the opportunity to develop robust networking connections with the individuals who contribute comments to your forum.

5. Participate in Social Activities with Owners of Other Businesses. You will have the opportunity to meet many potential customers at business meetings. Participate in industry events and conferences to expand your professional network and meet other people who might be able to help your company grow through agreements that are favourable to both parties. You may create and keep your relationships by engaging in activities like playing golf, going to social or charitable events, and generally socializing with your network of contacts.

Send new customers an email in which you respond to any questions they may have or offer to meet with a new prospective customer at any convenient location to talk and expound on business-related concerns. This helps to develop a lasting partnership between the two companies. Make sure to follow up on any emails you send with a phone call to solidify further and build your relationship.

6. Do not forget your returning customers. Your frequent and devoted customers deserve extra appreciation and consideration at all times. Your existing customers bring in more revenue for your company than new customers. Your previous customers are well aware of your capabilities and will come to you for assistance whenever they have a need.

The bond between you and your most loyal consumers will be strengthened if you provide them exclusive discounts and services. It is not required to solely give advantages relevant to the company's operation. You might provide vouchers for any unique social gathering, concerts, or forthcoming celebrations and access to nearby sights. You can also send birthday cards and greetings to other key events like anniversaries and graduations.

7 . Keep your flexibility and learn to overcome challenges. Always keep an open mind to keep your business connections stable and fruitful. It takes contributions from many different individuals for a firm to be successful. These contributions can be from business partners, employees, mentors, customers, or even your contemporaries. In all your business contacts, under no circumstances should you underestimate somebody, and you should always have a courteous demeanour.

In the course of running your business, you might face a lot of challenges. By maintaining open lines of communication and having the ability to accommodate any delays, uncertainties, or upsets that may arise, you can cultivate a business connection that is amicable and productive with all of the people who are affiliated with your company as a whole.

Establishing solid connections with other business professionals is essential to achieving commercial success. In order to get people talking about your company, you need to focus on creating and maintaining your contact list, as well as participating in networking events. Your company will collapse if you do not increase the size of your consumer base and cultivate solid professional relationships with other entrepreneurs who may provide assistance to your company. Make use of the resources at your disposal, including email, your business card, your website, and the business services you offer, in order to strengthen your relationships with the business contacts you have.

Why Are Business Relationships So Important?

Relationships are so meaningful in business that you can't make a profit without them.

You will have to get to know many different kinds of people. Relationships with vendors, contractors, employees, clients, and customers are all part of running a business.

Some people say that relationships are one of your most valuable business assets.

They Build Trust: Relationships give you time to get to know someone and build trust, so you can do business with them without worrying. That doesn't mean you don't make contracts anymore, but it does mean that you know the agreement will be kept because of the relationship.

Strong relationships lead to success.

Studies show that people who connect with others and build strong relationships have a better quality of life and do better in life than those who don't.

Managing Relationships Takes Skill

In business, you will need to use many different parts of building relationships. This means having the right mindset, creating processes, and having various skills that will help you manage different kinds of relationships.

They Create plans and leaders.

When you realize that building relationships is part of becoming a leader, you can go much further than you ever thought possible, mainly because this is how people do best.

Relationships are an essential part of life, whether they are personal or for business.

Help You Manage Risk

Knowing someone before doing business is a great way to manage risk. Before doing business with someone, you're less likely to have problems if you've done your research and taken the time to get to know them.

When you build relationships with your audience, you can get to know them better and develop more valuable things for them. You will discover their problems from the inside, which will help you create more solutions and add more value for your customers.

The Right Connections Educate yourself.

Even if you don't believe it, the more people you meet and build relationships with, the more you can learn. It comes down to resources. You don't have to know everything. If you want to, you can surround yourself with smart people you can ask questions of. Not only that, but you can also find more trusted people to outsource to.

They make opportunities for partnerships better.

Joint ventures are one way to make more money. Short-term partnerships on different projects that you both have skills for can help you reach more people and make more money.

CHAPTER 8

GET YOUR CAREER ON TRACK

If you have seen the cable television show on Bravo called "Inside the Actors Studio," then you have seen host James Lipton ask his celebrity guests to respond to the Bernard Pivot questionnaire. This questionnaire includes two questions regarding what the guests would most like to do outside of their chosen profession, as well as what they would most not like to do outside of their chosen profession:

1. Aside from the one you currently hold, what other line of work would you like to try?

2. Is there a certain kind of work that you would prefer to avoid?

(For instance, Robin Williams would like to be a "Neurologist," but he would prefer not to be a "Bomb Tester." Similarly, Sarah Jessica Parker would like to own a grocery store, but she would prefer not to be a "Chicken Plucker.")

It is crucial to determine both the jobs that you consider to be your "dream jobs" and the jobs that you consider to be your "nightmare jobs." Doing so helps you begin to think about what you want and do not want in a career.

What sets a career apart from a job, or do they really go hand in hand at all?

One definition of the term "career" is "a chosen pursuit," while another describes it as "the overall path or advancement of your working life or your professional achievements." Your job title is less important than the process that leads up to it, and your career is more about the path you take than the destination you reach. Jobs are typically an integral element of your ongoing goal or growth, and most of us have more than one job during the course of our careers.

How do you advance your career or make it stronger?

Developing your career is the strategy you use to move forward in the direction you wish to go with your professional life. It is "the strategic acquisition over time of the knowledge, attitudes, and skills you need to 1) meet the needs of your employer and 2) reach your personal long-term work-life goals." Career development can be defined as "the strategic acquisition over time of the knowledge, attitudes, and skills you need."

Even if our job should be about what we want, it should also be about what the demands of our employer are. In order to advance, it is necessary for us to continually increase the value we provide to our company and to keep our marketability in this increasingly competitive environment. If we are unable to fulfill the responsibilities for which we were employed, no employer "owes" us a job. Because we've been at this job for a while doesn't mean our employer 'owes' us a promotion. It is up to us to achieve success in our careers.

Either you have the goal of establishing a long-term career path with your current job or you have more immediate goals in mind. During the course of this workshop, we will take an objective look at the various career paths available to you and discuss the steps you can take to improve your chances of achieving your professional objectives, either inside or outside of your current place of employment.

Why should your employer be concerned about how your career is progressing? Why not just concentrate on how well you are performing in the short term at your current job?

Because it makes sense. In order to maintain a competitive edge in a sector that is notoriously cutthroat, your company must excel at recruiting and retaining top talent. As a result, the company has the goal of ensuring the success, contentment, and further growth of each and every employee. People who are aware of what they want to accomplish in their professions down the road and who believe that they are making progress toward that goal are more likely to perform at high levels in the here and now.

You should always be asking yourself these three questions if you want to develop a successful career: Where am I now?

Where do I want to be? Where do I need to be?

How exactly am I going to get there?

I don't want to give the impression that you should be dissatisfied with the work that you're doing right now (I hope you love your work and feel that it is fulfilling enough to be considered a significant part of your career aspirations). On the other hand, you need to have a strategy that is both progressive and continuing in order to increase your employable talents and get yourself closer to having a successful long-term career.

Seven errors that will cause your career to come to an abrupt halt (and How to Fix It)

As you move up in your career, it's common to plan out your next step and figure out what assignment, project, or job will help you reach your career goals. Still, no matter how hard we try, we sometimes make mistakes that throw off even the best career plans. Here are seven (7) mistakes that will destroy your career and how to fix them.

1. Not being willing to learn

Our world is not always the same. Things are constantly changing, so there are always new technologies, new ways to do something, and new ways to connect with customers. You could be left out if you don't learn more about these changes, how they affect your organization, and what it takes to manage or lead in these conditions.

Fix-it Strategy: Make a fixed time in your schedule for learning. This will help you develop a strong desire to learn. Find out what has changed in your job, your business, and your market, and make changes to how you manage or lead based on what you learn.

2: Making people doubtful

Trust is the glue that holds relationships between managers and employees or between people in general. You make people doubt you when you act in different ways or don't do what you say you'll do.

Fix-it Strategy: Make sure you always believe you will keep your word. When you make a promise, you should keep it. When you make a promise, keep it.

3. Not being aware of politics

Politics can't be avoided in organizations. Each organization is a living system with different groups of people who care about other things. If you don't do these things, you could end up in a career desert. Managers often make mistakes when they say or do something without thinking about how it will affect the people around them.

Fix-it Strategy: Work hard to understand how your organization works, and talk with your coach about how to avoid possible pitfalls.

4. Putting all your hopes in just one "mentor."

Many professionals, managers, and leaders rely on one person to help them with their careers, projects, or interests. This is a risky plan for more than one reason. The mentor might not have enough power to help you get where you want to go in your career or with your project. Second, if you only have one mentor, you can only grow and move up through his or her network of influence.

Fix-it Strategy: Build a large, responsive network of mentors and advisors who can help you find growth and advancement opportunities.

5. You don't have key job-related skills to do your job well.

When you get a new job, get a promotion, move to a new division, or get more responsibilities, you may need to learn new skills to do well in your new role. If you don't have a key skill or talent that you need to do the job well, you could get a low score on your next performance review.

Fix-it Strategy: Make a list of the skills you need to do your job, and then learn them as quickly as you can.

6. Not putting together a team.

Most managers and leaders are successful because they were good as individuals. Few people did well because of what they did on a team. Because of this, not many people know how to put together good teams. Teams can help with tasks that need help from many different parts of a business, like putting in place new systems or making new products. If you don't put together a team, you might not be able to get the results you're responsible for.

Strategy to fix it: There are many ways to build a team that works well together. Start by figuring out how much your team, or any team, is worth based on what each member brings to the table. Learn skills that will help you lead your team better.

7. Problems with the way the job was done

Poor performance is the biggest threat to a person's career. When you consistently miss goals and targets, it hurts your performance. If you don't always do a good job, you probably won't get new, more difficult jobs or be promoted. Even worse, persistent problems with performance could lead to being fired.

CHAPTER 9

THE INFLUENCE OF YOUR ATTITUDE ON YOUR BUSINESS OUTCOMES

What prompted you to leap into entrepreneurship in the first place? Have you become weary of your corporate work and believe that you might perform it more effectively? Are you at home with your family while also running a business you started as a hobby? Have you lost your job all of a sudden and are in need of a new source of income?

All too frequently, I hear from my customers that they are putting in excessive effort in their businesses but are not noticing an improvement in profits. If you needed to make extra money, how quickly do you think you could achieve it? The majority of the time, we limit ourselves in some way. You talk a good game about establishing a great business, but some of the measures you need to do are downright terrifying. You are avoiding things as a result of your fear, but you aren't even aware that this is happening to you.

Shawna is a person who organizes things. She was able to come into a client's home or business and effortlessly transform the space for them. She was eager to expand her company, but after some reflection, she recognized that she was not taking advantage of chances.

She assisted her customers in being more organized. She was aware of the gratitude her customers felt toward her. She didn't fully appreciate her talent, despite having a lot of passion for what she did and could do it all day long. She struggled to make ends meet at the end of the month and continued to work. Shawna stated that she desired success, but something was preventing her from achieving it.

You have to understand that Shawna held contradictory beliefs. She desired to be successful but had no interest in becoming wealthy. Her attitudes about financial matters prevented her from increasing her salary above a particular threshold. After looking at the data, it was clear that she had maintained the same income level for several years. This was not based on anything that actually occurred. This came about as a result of a self-created misconception held by Shawna. What happened to her is something that might happen to any one of us.

When we were younger, our experiences shaped the beliefs that we hold today. If you hold views that directly oppose your current objectives, then progress will either be completely halted or will be tough to achieve. Even worse, it might result in some sort of sabotage.

Thankfully, one's beliefs can evolve over time. It is possible to change your thinking on your own, but it might be challenging to do so. You become so accustomed to seeing things in a particular manner that you become unable to change your perspective.

You don't have to put up with this if you don't want to. You will complete the process a lot more rapidly if you collaborate with someone else who is trained in addressing mental difficulties and who is aware of how to assist in the creation of breakthroughs. Sometimes all you need is the assistance of another person to get you to think outside the box and take a look at things from a different angle.

As can be seen, Shawna was putting roadblocks in front of her own progress. Her mental game and attitude toward money were harming her objectives for professional achievement. She was holding herself back because she felt that having more money went against who she was as a person. She would morph into a different person if she achieved an excessive level of achievement and had an excessive amount of wealth. Her net worth wouldn't improve until she changed the way she thought about money, so until then, it would stay the same.

At first, Shawna was hesitant to agree to a price increase for her services. She was under the impression that people would not be willing to pay more for her services. While we were concentrating on increasing her prices, she came to the conclusion that she would not pay such rates herself, so why should she expect anybody else to pay that price? Shawna came to the conclusion that her problems stemmed from a lack of self-worth.

Shawna was able to gain an understanding of how her limiting attitude was preventing her from achieving her goals as she began to recognize some of her key beliefs. She needed to investigate her beliefs and the ways in which those ideas influenced both her perceptions and her actions. Those that did not help her achieve her objectives for the growth of her company were investigated even more. It was discussed that there are new alternate points of view. She may now move forward in a number of different ways. After she overcame her initial reluctance, she started to recognize the opportunities.

Shawna came up with a strategy to increase her fees that she was happy with and implemented it. She freely confesses that the increase in her rates was a "gulp" for her to take. In point of fact, she was instructed to take a substantial sip before revealing her rates, and then she was supposed to wait for a response. It was both terrifying and wonderful when she got her first client at her increased prices.

Things started going in a positive direction. Without any more effort on her part, Shawna began to experience an improvement in her income. Shawna continued to focus on her mental approach to taking those subsequent major steps toward achieving her goals. If she were the only person responsible for her achievement, she would continue to struggle with it. She was astonished at how simple it could be after working with another person to establish new beliefs that suited the goals she had set for herself.

Completely unexpected things frequently occur. That is just the way life is. Do you have the mentality to move beyond your comfort zone and do things differently in order to achieve the things you want to? If you want to be successful, you have to convince yourself that you are already successful. It's all about your frame of mind. As soon as you start to challenge yourself and think beyond the box, the response from your company will follow suit.

Get a piece of paper and divide it into two columns for this activity. In the left column, give it the heading "Values," and then list all of the qualities and strengths that correspond to those values that you possess. Move your cursor on the word "Actions" to the right. The "Pros" section will take up the upper half of the Actions section. These steps you're taking right now will help your company reach the next level of success and become more successful overall. After that, compose the

"Cons" section. The actions you do, as a result, prevent the expansion of your company.

When that is finished, go to the following step, which is to write next to each Action, the pros and the cons, which value each Action supports. Check whether there is a pattern once you have matched each Action with a corresponding value first. This can help you identify the areas in which your values are at odds with one another, which is the first step in comprehending why you might be preventing your company from expanding.

Home Business Opportunity: Letting Go of the Extra Weight to Succeed

Even though many people like the idea of a "home business," most fail within the first year. In this article, I'd like to discuss a few things you might need to get rid of if you want your home business to succeed.

Fear is the number one reason most people fail at their home-based businesses. People are afraid to use new ideas and strategies in their companies, even when the ones they already use don't work. They stick to what has worked in the past because they don't know what would happen if the new plan failed.

For a business to be successful, it has to do something that has never been done before. If you keep doing the same things over and over, you will get the same or worse results because you won't be the only one doing them, and there will be many other people doing them too. If you try new ideas, you'll get different results.

Doubt: The exact opposite of confidence is doubt. Many people fail at their home-based business because they don't believe in their own ability to run it. Will I be able to do well when I'm up against so much competition? This is the most common doubt people have, even if they have the talent and skills to succeed.

If you have doubts about the quality of your own product, you won't be able to show it to your customers with confidence. So, neither your sales nor your income will go up. This will make you doubt yourself even more.

On the other hand, if you're sure of yourself, people are more likely to listen to you and invest in your ideas. This will help you make more money and boost your confidence.

Focusing too much on productivity:

Why do you need to work quickly and well?

It would help if you had it because it helps you work faster, makes more sales, and makes more money. The whole point of efficiency is to get more done in less time. But to be as productive as possible, many people pay less attention to the quality of their work. When you look at life as a whole, quality, not quantity, brings in the most work.

How to Use Your Skills to Succeed in a New Line of Work

Today, with the world being so interconnected, it is usual to speak multiple languages. People study foreign languages for various reasons, including as a hobby, to work overseas, or both.

Knowing more than one language can be a tremendous advantage and enable us to produce passive income by acting as an internet translators and addressing our own needs.

Although most people can comprehend English, people have acknowledged the need to try to communicate with those who cannot. According to research, if this language barrier can be overcome, many internet firms have the potential to expand significantly. As a result, there is a significant market demand for content translated into numerous languages. Web browsers can also display content in many languages according to the user's location.

Knowing other languages can help you land jobs translating content from one language to another in this vibrant market. The majority of these initiatives focus on translating content from English into other languages. The first step in starting this method for generating residual income would be to enrol in a course and gain a thorough knowledge of the languages you already know. Only if you can demonstrate some credentials or your prior work will clients looking for translators be interested in your profile.

You can sign up and submit bids for translation assignments in numerous places. Most of these services are paid per word, and you can determine the price your clients would take according to how frequent or unusual a language is. According to the trend, most customers want translation services into languages like Spanish, French, Chinese, and Russian, among others. Even if we may be native speakers of these languages, it is another thing to translate into the local dialect while maintaining the spirit and meaning of the original text.

Many resources can help you make money doing translation work on the Internet. One tool that can assist you in finding words if you get stuck is Google Translate. It is up to your judgment to choose the term that fits in the sentence and maintains the intended meaning, even though internet translator programs can assist you in finding a list of words that mean the same in the language you are translating to. Your online reputation would grow with each job you completed, opening up more opportunities for you to work as a translator and produce a steady flow of passive revenue.

.

CHAPTER 10

THE SECRETS TO TURNING YOUR HOBBIES INTO PROFITABLE ONLINE BUSINESSES

There are, in fact, a great number of people who have made a significant amount of money from their pastimes. The wonderful thing about this is that these people get to engage in activities that they take pleasure in while at the same time earning a respectable sum of money on the side. If others have complimented the items that you have developed in your spare time, it is perhaps time for you to think about starting an online business. But before you go ahead and accomplish that, there are a few things that you need to first take into consideration:

Market Appeal

It is critical to investigate whether or not there is a market for the product you are developing. If you do not have someone interested in purchasing your goods, your time and effort will likely be wasted. It is very recommended that you carry out some primary market research. This may entail determining whether or not people will pay money for your product, how much they are willing to pay for it, how large your market is, and how you may develop ways to market and sell your product at an affordable price. If the results of your research indicate that marketing and selling your goods on the internet would result in a profit, then you should pursue this avenue.

Expectations That Are True to Reality

Your company's success is directly proportional to your ability to define and pursue goals and objectives based on reality. You must have an understanding of the benefits and drawbacks associated with beginning an internet business. To start, you need to decide whether you will be pursuing your endeavour on a part-time or full-time basis. Most of your time will be taken up by internet businesses that originated as hobbies because you will also be responsible for managing the business side of things. It is highly recommended that you develop a business plan detailing all the potential expenses associated with operating your internet-based business. It would help if you now had a better understanding of how much time you will need to devote to secure your success. If you have a high level of enthusiasm for your pastime and everything appears to be in order on paper, you might want to consider taking the plunge and launching an online business.

Marketing That Gets Results

Speaking of taking chances, you should be aware that even if you are skilled and talented, your internet business will never be successful if it has no paying customers. When it comes to securing the success of a company, marketing is an essential component. One option available to you is to sell your wares via your very own website. However, to increase the number of potential clients you attract, you will need an efficient marketing approach that does not spend a lot of money.

Affiliate marketing is where you should focus your efforts in this situation. Many online companies are turning to affiliate marketing to sell more of their products and take up a more significant portion of their market share. As its name suggests, affiliate marketing will involve other people, known as affiliates, who will essentially be responsible for marketing and selling your products. You may find many companies that offer affiliate marketing services because the popularity of such a marketing method has already swept across the community of businesses that operate on the internet.

Know The Real Causes Of Business Failure With These Business Strategies For Success

Inadequate money, poor organization, and inadequate marketing are some of the most evident factors contributing to a business's collapse. These are simple to recognize and, ideally, steer clear of. However, there are more, far less obvious reasons that most business owners are unaware of.

They are under the impression that they are doing everything correctly, but their performance continues to fall significantly short of expectations. They are left wondering what could possibly be wrong as they watch their dreams vanish before their eyes.

Failure in business is far more often than it should be, particularly if you are aware of the factors that contribute to its occurrence.

1.   You have the incorrect motivations for starting your own firm. If money is your primary motivation, you need to be quite certain about why that is the case. It is essential that you have

a powerful emotional attachment to the reason why you choose to engage in that particular line of work in the first place.

2. Either an excessive amount of information or an insufficient amount of understanding regarding the processes involved in operating a firm. You will have a difficult time if you do not have sufficient knowledge. When faced with an excessive amount of information, some people experience feelings of being overwhelmed. It's possible that you feel as though you need to have every question answered before you can move on. Remember that you only need to know sufficient information to achieve your desired results. Everything else is merely information that can be picked up along the way.

3. The irrational fear of failing. It is not about what it will do to you but about the notion that this is your only opportunity for success in this particular endeavour. If you are unsuccessful, you will have wasted that one chance. You decide to cling to the dream rather than pursue the chance provided to you because you do not want to run the danger of having the dream slip away.

4. The fear of being successful. This may sound strange to you, given that you went into business to be successful; yet, if that is the case, why would you allow your fear of success to lead to losing your firm? You have to be honest about how you feel about success and having a lot of money. How does it make you feel to know that you can have everything? Or do you believe that it may be more than you deserve?

If you address each of these issues, you will be well on rescuing your floundering company.

Becoming an idea generator is one option available to you. Create several different aspirations for yourself so that if one of them does not come true, you have a number of other options available.

You should jot down each new idea and develop business strategies for them, including how you would make money, where it would come from (various revenue streams), how to get customers and traffic, what you will offer, and how you will expand on your main idea in the future. Write down each new statement and develop business strategies for them.

In addition, jot down all the reasons why you deserve to be successful and live the lifestyle you envision for yourself. Include your unique skills and what makes you happy now and when you were younger, and be specific about what it is that you have to give. It would help if you considered seeking feedback from someone you can rely on because other people are typically able to see something in you that you do not notice in yourself.

CHAPTER 11

THE 30 BEST SOURCES OF PASSIVE INCOME AND IDEA FOR WEALTH CREATION

Despite claims to the contrary, most lucrative passive income concepts result from labourintensive processes such as audience development, paid ad optimization, and the provision of first-rate services and products.

But you're not scared to put in the time to do all those things, and you might already have all three crossed off your list as a current or aspiring business owner.

You may have more freedom, adaptability, and money if you add passive income sources to your life. With examples and advice to get you started, learn 30 different passive income streams.

How does passive income work?

Active unearned income from a source other than regular employment and requires little work to develop and sustain referred to as passive income.

Investments in mutual funds, online product sales, online website course delivery, and other non-participatory side jobs are examples of passive income sources.

With little time and effort, passive income generates unearned residual money. You'll have more time, and your money will be better off. The stress and anxiety associated with exchanging your time for money can be lessened, and you may feel more secure about your financial future.

Investigate the following passive revenue ideas, whether you're a service provider wishing to quit selling money for hours or a product company looking to add income sources that don't require the logistics of sending out real things.

30 ways to make money using passive income

1. Open a drop shipping store.

Drop shipping is one of the best ways to start making money right away, no matter where you are or how much money you have. Some drop shippers say that they make more than $100,000 a year. Drop shipping is not a quick way to get rich, but it does take some time to set up.

With this business model, you set up an online store where people can look at products and buy them. Drop shipping is interesting because you don't have to see the products you sell in person.

With drop shipping, your supplier takes care of everything, from making the product to packing it and sending it to the customer. And there's not much cash risk because you don't have to send money to your supplier until your customers pay.

You also don't have to worry about the risk of investing in a product that no one wants. You can find popular products in different niches to sell in your store by using a platform like the DSers.

You can make a good passive income and learn how to run an ecommerce business, depending on the product you choose and how much you charge for it.

2. Open a store that prints on demand

If you are an artist, a designer, or a business owner, "print on demand" can be a good way to make passive income and sell your work. It involves working with suppliers to customize white-label products like t-shirts, posters, backpacks, and books and selling them on a perorder basis.

Like dropshipping, you only pay for the product after it has been sold. There's no need to buy in bulk or keep an inventory. Print-on-demand stores are a good way to make passive income because: you can make products quickly and sell them in minutes; your supplier handles shipping and fulfillment; once your store is set up, you can automate many marketing and sales tasks;

With a print-on-demand company like Printful, you can quickly make products to sell in your Shopify store. Overall, print on demand is a simple business idea with low risk that you can start up quickly.

3. Sell digital products

Upfront time investment (time): Upfront money investment (money): Potential for passive income:

Digital products are assets or media that people can't touch with their hands. These are things like Kindle books, templates, plug-ins, or PDFs that can be downloaded or streamed.

Digital products with high profit margins are great ways to make money while you sleep. You only have to make the asset once to sell it online over and over again. There's no need to store or keep track of anything.

You can sell an unlimited number of digital products. Many creators increase their passive income by selling kits, printables, files, and other assets that professionals can use. For example, UX Kits sells personas, flowcharts, and wireframes to help with design.

4. Give online lessons

Online course sales are easier than ever for teachers. You can easily make courses and start selling them, whether they are about marketing, illustration, or business. Like digital products, you can sell online courses over and over again without having to keep any stock or inventory.

To teach online, you have to put in some time at the beginning. You'll need to plan out your course, record it, and give students things they can take with them, like templates.

Take Yegi Saryan, who started the company Yegi Beauty. After making an online beauty brand that sells eyelash extension products, she made Yegi Academy, which is an educational branch. Her online and in-person lash classes help entrepreneurs all over the world get their beauty careers off the ground.

As an online teacher, you can decide how big your class is and how long it lasts. If you like working with small groups, you could offer one-on-one tutoring or masterminds. If you like working with big groups, you could offer training sessions and live courses. Don't want to talk to people? No problem. You can make courses that students can download and work on at their own pace.

No matter how you look at it, teaching online is a good way to make money without doing much work. You only need to invest your time.

5. Become a blogger

Starting a blog can be hard, but as a passive income stream, it is becoming more and more popular as a business model. You no longer have to be a big name on the internet to make money online. All you have to do is find your people on one or two platforms and send them to your website.

Building a blog takes a little bit of time. But if you make good content and share it on your platforms, you'll build a big enough audience to make money from it.

You could make passive income from blogging by: selling affiliate products, writing sponsored posts, selling your own products, or running ads through Google AdSense.

What's the best? To start a blog, you don't need to know how to design or code. You can get a blog up and running quickly with a content management system and hosting service like Shopify.

You will need to spend time making an SEO marketing plan, making content, and promoting it. Know that your hard work will pay off.

Depending on how you make money from your blog, the return on investment can be as high as $30,000 per month.

6. Sell handmade goods

Selling things online has never been easier. Since more than 4.6 billion people are connected to the internet, there are a lot of chances to start and grow an online business.

There are a lot of places online where you can sell things. Some specialize in certain things, like video games or hand-made goods, while others let you sell anything.

Some of the most popular places to sell things online are:

Handshake.com. Amazon.com. eBay.com. Ruby Lane.com. AliExpress.com.

There are two parts to the initial investment. To make and sell things like pottery or clothes that you make yourself, you'll need to spend money on materials and time. You should also set up an online store to sell your goods.

7. Run a business based on affiliate marketing

Affiliate marketing involves telling people about a product or service. It's a great way to make passive income because when someone uses your referral link to buy the product or service you suggested, you get a commission.

This is also a growing business. Statista thinks that by 2022, the affiliate marketing market will be worth $8.2 billion. Affiliate marketing is a way for online business owners to make money.

- It's simple to do. You only have to worry about marketing. The brand will make products and ship them to customers.

- The risk is low. Affiliate programs are free to join. You can sell already-made money without having to pay money up front. So that more people click on your links, you'll have to spend time making traffic sources. Once that is set up, you can make money through commissions that are mostly passive. Most affiliate marketers don't hire anyone else to help them. You can tell people about new products and make campaigns while your old work is still making money in the background.

Affiliate marketing can be a great way to make money and bring in more money for your business. Only your time is needed. Once you've put in the time, you can keep getting the benefits.

8. Use the web to sell stock photos

The fact that you get paid for your time is one of the worst things about running a service-based business like photography. To make money with photography, you have to be at an event or photoshoot. Even if you're making a lot of money, this can get old after a while.

If you are a photographer full-time or have a good camera, you can make extra money by selling photos online. Stock photo sites like

Pexels and Shutterstock will pay for good photos and videos, as will other online media companies.

Only your camera and laptop are the only things you need to keep around the house. Once you upload your photos to these sites, they will market and sell them for you.

If you run your photography business on Shopify, it's easy to add digital products like prints or print-on-demand products like shirts and hats. This gives you even more passive income streams so you can work less and make more.

9. Become a big name on Instagram

Dwayne "The Rock" Johnson makes $1 million for every Instagram post he makes. Even if you don't have chiseled abs or more than 200 million followers on social media, you can still make passive income as an influencer on Instagram.

To become an Instagram influencer—someone who can persuade someone else to buy something—you'll need to build a group of people who like the same things you do.

Are you a comics fan? You can sign up for Instagram and post regularly about the latest Marvel and DC shows. The same is true if you like sports, scuba diving, decorating your home, or even learning about other cultures.

10. Buy a place to rent out

If you have enough money, you can buy apartment buildings or other types of real estate and then rent them out. But since being a landlord is a pretty busy job, you can hire property managers to take care of your tenants and get the rent each month.

What if you don't have enough money to buy a whole building of apartments? Can you still make money from renting? Yes, you can.

With a minimum investment of $500, you can use a real estate investment trust (REIT) platform like Fundrise to invest in different real estate assets and earn passively when the assets go up in value.

11. Put your money into the stock market

Even though the stock market can be hard to understand and has a steep learning curve, it's a great way to build long-term wealth. Most people make the mistake of thinking in the short term when they should be thinking in the long term to reach their financial goals.

When you buy stocks, your goal is to diversify your portfolio and lower your risk. You can do this by putting your money into exchange-traded funds (ETFs) and stocks with high dividends that give you a steady stream of income over time. You need to open a brokerage account and put money into it before you can start investing in the stock market.

12. Rent out your spare room

Does your apartment have a spare room? Or are you going on a three-week road trip and don't want your house to be empty while you're gone? You can rent out your extra space by working with a rental company like Airbnb.

Airbnb puts homeowners in touch with people who are looking for a place to stay for their next vacation. People like Airbnbs because they are usually cheaper than hotels. This means that as an Airbnb host, there is a high demand for your free space.

If you want to make even more money with Airbnb, you could buy apartments just to rent them out. You should know, though, that renting out your space usually means you have to do some work first. You might have to buy furniture or fix up the room before you can rent it out.

13.   Rent out your car Time investment up front (time): Money investment up front (money):

You can make passive income from more than just your free space. You can also use a service like Turo to rent out your car. If you already use your car for Uber, you can sign up with platforms like Carvertise or Wrapify to make extra money while driving around town. You could also look for someone who wants to use your car for Uber or Lyft. So when you don't have anything to do, you can put on a Netflix show and let your car do the work.

14. Give money to your friends

Upfront time investment (time): Upfront money investment (money): Potential for passive income:

Have extra money that isn't making you any money? As a side job, you could try peer-to-peer lending. P2P lending is when people or small businesses borrow money from other people. Sign up on a site like LendingClub, Prosper (for individuals), or Worthy (for businesses) that connects borrowers and lenders to make the process easier.

Most of the time, these sites have loan requests and interest rates that are based on the borrower's past. Most of the time, the return on these loans is between 5% and 6%.

15. Make money while you shop online

When you shop online, you can get cash back from sites like Swagbucks, MyPoint, and Rakuten. You don't have to do anything else to make money on these sites besides sign up and shop. You get more points the more you shop online. And you can make more money.

16. Websites can be bought and sold.

There are a lot of websites about just about anything you can think of. What's the best? Many of them make a good living from affiliates, ads, memberships, or selling products, and they are often for sale.

17. Start a YouTube channel

You can still make a YouTube channel. 74% of adults in the United States use YouTube. That's a lot of people to earn money from without doing anything. What is it? It takes a lot of work up front with little or no payoff at first.

But if you think long-term and don't mind putting in more work at the beginning, a successful YouTube channel can bring in a lot of money. Affiliate sales, sponsorships, branded integrations, and ad income can all add up passively as you add content, clicks, and views and grow your audience.

18. Invest in real estate investment trusts

A real estate investment trust, or REIT, is a company that owns and manages real estate that makes money. It's a great way for small investors to pool their money and buy investments that they couldn't buy on their own.

In the last ten years, REIT investments had an average annual return of 9.5%. REITs are a good way to make passive income over the long term and are worth looking into if you have enough money to get started.

To get started, you need money up front and to do a lot of research. You don't want to go into this investment blind. This guide is just one of the many things you can use to help you get started.

19. Bet on digital currencies

Investing in multiple cryptocurrencies, also known as "staking crypto," is a great way to earn between 5% and 10% passively. You can compare it to getting interest on your savings, but the returns are higher.

How do you get started? First, you should learn about proof-of-stake cryptocurrencies and how to get a cryptocurrency wallet. Then you'll need to learn about the different coins you can buy so you can choose the best one to invest in. When you're ready, you can buy crypto on crypto exchanges like Kraken or Coinbase.

After that, all you have to do is wait for your investments to pay off and check on them every so often. The more you learn about the world of crypto, the better decisions you'll make about where to invest.

Keep in mind that staking crypto has its own risks, just like any other investment. You'll also need to spend a lot of time at the beginning learning about your options so you can make smart investments.

20. Sell designs online

Upfront time investment (time): Upfront money investment (money): Potential for passive income:

You can sell digital designs online on sites like 99designs, ThemeForest, and Creative Market. Whether you use a website builder to make website themes, logos, branding resources, templates, illustrations, or even fonts, these platforms already have a market of people looking for design resources.

Graphic design is a $13.1 billion business in the US, and it's only getting bigger. Gladly, it's also easy to get a piece of that pie by doing nothing.

For example, if you wanted to start selling designs on Creative Market, you would have to apply and wait for approval. From there, you'll have your own storefront where you can start selling your branded designs.

21. Put your money in businesses

Today, you can start investing in business opportunities that were hard to get to in the past. With a $100 initial investment and no investor fees, it is easy to invest passively on platforms like Mainvest.com.

The profits? It depends, as with any investment. But Mainvest aims to give you between 10% and 25% back. Even better, you don't have to check out the businesses yourself. Mainvest checks out the business for you. You just have to put up the money to get started.

This is a great idea for passive income and a safe way to start investing in businesses and learn as you go.

22. Rent out the space you're not using

Have a room or garage that's empty and you're not using? Rent it out as a place to keep things! With storage rental platforms like Neighbor, Peerspace, and StoreAtMyHouse, you can do this in a safe and efficient way.

By 2026, the storage industry could be worth as much as $64 billion. In other words, this is not a way to make money without doing anything. You can store many different things, like cars, boats, RVs, and even business inventory.

Using storage rental platforms is also a great way to avoid liability issues because they offer safe payment options, contracts, and information about both the storage provider and the client.

23. Sell NFTs Upfront time investment

Non-fungible tokens, or NFTs, are unique assets that are saved on a digital ledger. The great thing about NFTs is that the asset you store can be worth something. You can make NFTs for anything, including digital designs, photos, music, games, GIFs, and even videos.

It's simple to make an NFT. You can create an account on platforms like OpenSea and follow the step-by-step process for minting (which involves some additional gas fees).

Even though the NFT industry is still pretty new, sales have soared past the $10 billion mark. Still, you can still get into the space. Just know that creating NFTs that will sell requires an initial investment of time and money in the form of minting fees.

24. Create a job board

As an online entrepreneur, a job board is a great way to make passive income. Employers use these websites to let job seekers know about open positions. People looking for work can look for jobs online or in person. You can charge employers to post jobs on your job board and offer extra features like sponsored jobs or unlimited access to your candidate database.

Even if you don't want to start from scratch, you can buy a theme for a job board and start from there. Now, it's easy to make the website. Most of the work is in letting people know about your job board.

Once you get the flywheel going and people start coming back to your job board, a big chunk of your income will be passive. You can get ideas from sites like ProBlogger, Dribble, or Construction Jobs.

25. Create no-code apps

With today's "no-code" tools, even a beginner can make a simple to advanced app. Platforms like Appy Pie, Adalo, or Bubble make it possible to get started in an industry that had 218 billion downloads in 2020 alone.

To start, you'll have to decide whether you want to make a website or a mobile app. Aside from the idea for the app (what niche it will serve and what problem it will solve), you also need to think about how you will make money from it.

Apps can make money through: subscriptions; ads; pay-to-download; a marketplace model; and ads.

If you aren't sure what your app should be about, here is a great list of research tools to help you get started.

26. Write a digital guide

Most likely, you know a lot about a subject that people are willing to pay for. Try writing digital guides using what you know. It's easy to get started, and in many cases, you don't even have to put money down right away.

Time is what you will need to invest. Spend some time finding out what people are looking for. Google's suggestions can be a great place to start. With tools like Ubbersuggest, you can find out which keywords get a lot of searches.

From there, it's just a matter of setting up your digital guide to collect sales, either through your own storefront or a seller platform.

27. Get money from inventions.

There are still inventors today. With your unique ideas, you can make passive income. It's not often talked about, but this is a real way to make money without doing anything.

Starting is probably one of the hardest parts of being an inventor. You want to make sure you have a good invention that is useful and solves a problem. Check the US patent website first to make sure that your idea hasn't already been made.

Sites like Invention City and InventMyIdea can help you get started if you want to sell your invention outright. Depending on the deal you make, once your idea is on the market, you can get a share of the money it makes or a payment.

28. Record books on tape

Someone has to create audiobooks. Why can't you be that someone? Once you get into the business, you can make passive income through royalties, which is how most audiobook narrators get paid.

There are a few things you need to learn first if you want to make passive income from audiobooks. Learn how to audition, the right way to tell a story, where you'll work, and some editing skills.

You don't have to do it by yourself. Some platforms make it easier to get started and find your first few gigs. Check out sites like ACX to find out what you need to know to make it in the industry.

29. Invest in vending machines

Upfront financial investment (money): Upfront time investment (time): Passive income potential:

Ever wonder who takes care of all the vending machines that are always stocked? The person who owns those machines is making (semi) passive money off of your cravings for snacks and soda.

You can join in the fun by doing some research. Fun fact: The market for vending machines is worth a healthy $8.6 billion. And, like most other industries, it's set up to grow in the coming years.

Starting a passive income stream with vending machines does require an initial investment of time and money. This is a great guide with tips on how to get your first vending machine up and running.

Marketplaces like Craigslist, eBay, and BizBuySell can help you figure out how much money you'll need up front to buy your first set of machines (as well as how many you can afford to start). Once you find a place to put it, a vending machine route is a great way to make money that is mostly hands-off.

30. Create spreadsheets and sell them

Some of us are born knowing how to use spreadsheets. If this sounds like you, you can use your spreadsheet skills to make money while you sleep.

Whether you use Excel or Google Sheets to make spreadsheets, there are people who will pay you to make spreadsheets for budgeting, profit projections, tracking habits, or even P&L spreadsheets that business owners don't want to make from scratch.

With a Shopify storefront and the Digital Downloads app, you have a ready-to-go passive income stream. But you do need to get people to your storefront for that to happen. We're lucky to have some tools to help us with that.

CHAPTER 12

NO JOB? NOT A DIME? DO YOU UNDERSTAND THE MYTH RELATING TO THE PROVISION THAT "YOU NEED MONEY TO MAKE MONEY"

One of the oldest business fallacies is that you need money to make money. People without cash frequently cite it as a justification for why they haven't achieved financial success. You've heard these and other justifications; I wanted to do that deal, but I couldn't raise funds.

I knew it would be a big deal, but I lacked the funds to participate.

I have a fantastic idea for a product that would bring in millions, but I lack the funds to launch it.

A few years ago, I could have purchased the property for half of what it is currently selling for.

I really wanted to be my own boss, but I was just not able to find the money to do it.

Poor people simply remain poor; only the wealthy make money.

To launch your own company, create a new product, or establish a new service, you must have money.

To all of those and related justifications, I say hogwash.

These stale justifications are used by people who are only deceiving themselves. They are the kind of people you should avoid spending time with since they aren't as smart as they believe and don't know everything.

You need to develop your ability to ask questions. If you feel awkward asking questions, don't bother going into business. It takes asking questions and getting answers to be in business and to make money. The solutions hold the secret to generating income.

Here is an easy illustration; If your neighbour is selling his old station wagon, for example, would you be ready to give me a commission if I could find a buyer for it? They'll concur. Keep your distance from your neighbour if they respond negatively since they don't understand business, sales, or money.

I was always trying to make money when I was younger. There was no allowance for me. I had to work for my money, which helped me develop a strong work ethic. I painted garages, manicured lawns, shovelled snow, and washed automobiles, along with many other tasks.

I once ran into a friend of my neighbour who lives next door, and he indicated that he was looking to sell a Citizen's Band radio he owned. The cost was $100, but if I could find a buyer, he would give me an additional $10.

I located a buyer within twenty-four hours and earned a ten-dollar cash commission. Ten dollars might not seem like much, but when I'm telling you this story, the minimum wage was only 85 cents per hour. I would have had to mow ten yards to make that much money.

I was thirteen years old then, but the lesson was more significant than the ten dollars in commission. The study found alternative ways to create money that paid better than what businesses were paying.

No product was purchased, no money was committed, and all that was needed to make money was a little time and a few chats. Cool!

You don't need money to make money, but I don't want you to mistake that for needing money to put a deal together. You don't need money to be in business, start a firm, purchase a house, or send your children to school. You need to learn how to obtain funds from other sources.

I would have made that deal if I could have raised funds. The first justification given above is this.

Which would you choose: one per cent of a significant transaction or zero per cent of zero deals?

Some people immediately declare they wouldn't invest their time and effort in a deal for just 1%. These are typically the knowledgeable individuals who lack financial resources.

What if the transaction costs ten billion dollars? The loser thinks about the one per cent, even though one per cent of ten billion dollars is merely ten million dollars.

"One per cent of one hundred people's work is preferable to one hundred per cent of my efforts," the speaker said. — J. Paul Getty

You would be fortunate to be involved in a trade like this in the first place if you don't have any money. Thus, you can begin with lesser transactions.

Let's consider the other side of the argument: I have a brilliant concept for a product that would make millions, but I lack the funds to launch it.

Over the years, I've heard several variations of this justification. It's all nonsense.

First and foremost, most of the "amazing ideas" that these people are spreading are actually terrible ideas. However, you can imagine how wonderful it would be to flaunt your "million dollars" ideas to everyone you meet. If you say it often enough and to enough people, some might start referring to you as the person with all the excellent ideas.

The lesson you learn in the actual world is this. Like a magnet draws iron filings, good ideas draw money. The truth is that most people lack the knowledge or the will to develop their ideas further out of fear that they would not be such good ideas after all.

Though it may be difficult to imagine, ideas are pursued by money, not the other way around. To put it more accurately, capital is constantly seeking the highest return.

So that you can better understand it and avoid wasting your time, allow me to elaborate on this "chasing money" phrase. We'll illustrate using this.

You have an idea for a home-based business but need $25,000 to get it off the ground. You know that your aunt has a sitting balance of $27,000 in her savings account.

To ask your aunt for the money would be a BAD idea. Why? Because your theory hasn't been confirmed, it's virtual all the money she has. It would be an insult to your character to even approach her, so be prepared for a NO.

However, you still require $25,000, so you go to a billionaire, explain your business proposal, and request the funding. Most likely, the Billionaire will decline your offer. It's not that he lacks funds; rather, the deal is simply too modest.

Because they are billionaires, billionaires don't have time for twenty-five thousand dollar deals. With all due respect, you must locate the best fishing pool.

I built a manufacturing business plan for a product I developed and contacted a few investors. I required 50,000 bucks. That contract is too tiny, Lazz; if you have something more significant and meatier, call me. I can still hear those words. The cash was elsewhere.

You don't need money, but you require a thorough business plan detailing how the funds will be spent. Do not be frightened by the word "business plan." There are a ton of tools available that you may use for free to build and write your plan. Consider the public library and the internet. You might possibly get some assistance in this area from the Small Business Administration of the United States government.

A business plan is just a written report on your goals that is well-organized, simple to read, simple to understand, and simple to evaluate. It is simply that. It's simple.

Finding out whether or not your plan makes sense is the best part of creating your business plan. You'll need to make a decision if, after working on a business plan for your new venture, you learn that you lose money on every unit you sell.

You can give up on the idea, rework it to make it more lucrative, or— a sometimes overlooked option—sell or license the idea to someone who is already running a company that is comparable to yours or one where your idea would fit in well.

You're missing the point if you don't believe that putting a deal together can be profitable. By connecting buyers and sellers and generating a commission, a real estate broker brings deals together. By bringing a buyer and a seller together, a brokerage firm can profit. A matchmaking agency charges a fee for locating your ideal soul partner.

Finding a buyer for a seller and a seller for a buyer is a good strategy to employ if you are jobless and have no money. Because people need to raise money, they're prepared to let goods go for a low price, and buyers are constantly seeking for a deal, it's easier to get engaged in this the slower the economy is. The bargain can be offered by you.

The justification that you don't have any money is no longer acceptable.

Nevertheless, you still require $25,000, don't you? You should target investors here. Even if it would be simpler to find a single investor with $25,000, you might be able to raise $1,000 from 25 friends and family members or $5,000 from five investors.

However, if you keep it small and limit it to just a few investors, it's really simple to achieve. The big deals entail investment bankers and millions of dollars in fees. I advise you to seek the counsel of an experienced business attorney if you need answers to investor issues because I have no idea where you are currently located or what the laws are there.

Collaborations are simple. Did you and your friends save up money as kids so you could purchase a candy bar or soda instead of settling for something you both didn't want?

You're almost there if you have a sound strategy that makes sense, is simple to follow, and doesn't cost a lot of money to participate. You must approach individuals aware of what an investor is and how they vary from a partner.

A partner undoubtedly has more control over daily operations than an investor does.

I've learned that investors are preferred over partners. A partner is forever unless you buy each other out, whereas an investor can be bought out over time. Just deciding who will purchase can be a little tricky.

What is your current defence?

Get the money you need to launch your own home-based business or another type of business if you need it.

To recap what I've been saying: If you see a piece of real estate listed for sale that you know is a good deal, quickly put together a one-page description outlining the advantages of purchasing it, the profit that may be anticipated, and the time frame. Next, approach a wealthy individual with interest in real estate and offer them a proposition in which they would put up the cash, and you would work on the transaction as partners, or in which they would pay you a fee for locating the deal.

Here's a suggestion that is superior to watching TV. Ask the local business owners (who typically have some money) if they are interested in purchasing anything in particular for a reasonable price. Inform them that you have an extensive network and know many people who constantly want to buy and sell stuff. He might try to sell you something from his back room, such as an outdated copier, a car, dead stock, a space heater, etc.

Have a garage or yard sale where you collect items from neighbours who tell you what they want to pay, mark the price, and pocket the difference. Yes, it takes a little work, but you are the one who is currently a little broken.

Sell the unnecessary items you have lying around the house to raise money and launch your home-based business. There is always something you can sell. You can get a second instance of whatever you once believed you couldn't part with once you've made a fortune.

You can make money by selling goods you don't need, things that other people don't need, and something that people are having trouble selling on their own.

Don't merely imagine your million-dollar concept if it is genuinely that big. Create a business plan and an action plan, then begin talking to potential investors (don't waste your time with those who are merely interested in seeing what you have).

You might be surprised to learn that while many bad deals are completed, not all good sales are. That is simply the way the presenting system operates. The agreement has a decent probability of going through if it appears to make sense and sounds good.

Avoid attempting to con people with a glitzy presentation about a project that you know will never materialize, won't produce the desired results, or will siphon cash from those who can't afford to lose it. That is simply incorrect and frequently illegal.

Raising money for your second, third, and other upcoming ventures will be simpler if you act morally and reasonably.

You no longer have any justifications for not starting a home-based business, at least not the financial one. If you reread this book, you'll see that it's not hard to raise some money to start.

It is and will require some time and effort, but if you're unemployed, have a part-time job, or have financial difficulties, this could be the road that changes everything.

Money never sleeps, so when you start is entirely up to you. How much you sleep is entirely up to you. Consider this: How much is the other person sleeping, who has already started obtaining the funds required to launch his home-based business.

CONCLUSION

In the business world of today, talented leaders all over the world are constantly faced with choices when it comes to their careers. There's a good chance that your competitors will regularly reach out to your key people with tempting offers. Do you constantly remind them of what you offer in terms of talent?

Costs of turnover

Staff turnover costs can significantly affect a business, directly through the cost of hiring new people and indirectly through the cost of conversion, lower productivity, and less motivated employees when good managers leave.

The best way to cut these costs is to build and improve your talent value proposition. This is everything that talent cares about when deciding whether to join or stay with a company.

Put together your case.

Before you start putting together or improving your talent value proposition,

here are some tips:

Know your readers: Before you start coming up with critical messages, find out about the people you want to reach. What do they look for in an employer? Who do they think are your most formidable rivals on the talent market? (you will be surprised to see they are not your closest competitors in regular business). Make sure you talk to both your current and future employees in depth.

Focus on what makes you different: Don't talk about what you want to offer in the future. Instead, talk about what is unique and what your current employees think is helpful. What makes them work for you right now? Usually, a talent value proposition has the following parts:

o   Pay and benefits are the base offer that should be the same as what your competitors give. But studies of what executives look for in a job show that this is not the most important thing.

o   What matters are the chances to grow as a person and, in a broader sense, the company's culture and values. Executives decide on job changes based on these two things. They take years to build, which makes them much harder to copy.

o   Spread your brand through all channels: Make sure to spread your employer's brand through a wide range of media, from the most obvious, like job ads, to the less obvious, like what interviewers say about the company to candidates. When working on employer branding, a common mistake is putting all your attention on potential new employees and forgetting about your current vital people.

o   Your company's brand should be closely tied to the talent value proposition. HR, Corporate Communications, and your marketing department must work together. A company that wants to grow will work as hard on its employer brand as it does on its corporate and consumer brands.

Case Study: How the Swedish Trade Council figures out what its talent is worth "The Swedish Trade Council gives you a wide range of options:

o   At the Swedish Trade Council, you have a role with a purpose since we make a big difference in Swedish trade and industry. o The Swedish Trade Council has a wide range of exciting jobs for you since we work with a wide range of clients and services.

o   Working for the Swedish Trade Council gives you great chances to learn and grow...

and will set you up well for your future career."

Made in United States
North Haven, CT
26 February 2023

33175503R00075